B-17 FLY|

FORTRESS
GROUPS
OF THE EIGHTH AIR FORCE

IN FOCUS

**RED
KITE**

ACKNOWLEDGEMENTS

Many photographs in this album have passed through various people before arriving with us so we apologise if the name of the original photographer of any photo is not listed.

CONTRIBUTORS

Mike Bailey
Marvin Barnes
Theo Boiten
Frederick L Carr
Coen Cornelissen
Tom Cushing
Abel L. Dolim
Bill Donald
Bill Espie
Mike Faley
Thomas J. Fitton
Robert M. Foose
Bill Gibbons
Colonel Harry D. Gobrecht
Larry Goldstein
Harry Holmes
Ab Jansen
Ron Mackay
Danny McGahan
Brian S. McGuire
Ian McLachlan
Joseph Minton
Orlo Natvig
Hugh K. Crawford
Don & Peggy Garnham
Douglas Hunt DSC*
Gus Mencow
Derek Smith
David J. Schmitt

Simon Parry
Cliff Pyle
Connie and Gordon Richards
Dr. George Rubin
Frank Sherman
Sam Sox
Graham & Anne Simons of GMS Enterprises
David Schmitt
Hans-Heiri Stapfer
Leslie G. Thibodeau
Thorpe Abbotts 100th BG Memorial Museum
Walt Truax
Geoff Ward
Truett L. Woodall Jr.
Pete Worby
Sam Young
Russell J. Zorn
Eric Swain
Danny McGahan
Charles Nekvasil
ww2images.com

First Published in 2004 by
Red Kite
PO Box 223
Walton on Thames
Surrey
KT12 3YQ
www.redkitebooks.co.uk

(c) 2004 Martin W Bowman

Design by Mark Postlethwaite GAvA
Colour Profiles by Mike Bailey

Printed in Malta

ISBN 0-9546201-0-0

B-17 FLYING FORTRESS GROUPS

OF THE
EIGHTH AIR FORCE

IN FOCUS

by
MARTIN W BOWMAN

profiles by
MIKE BAILEY

RED KITE

CONTENTS

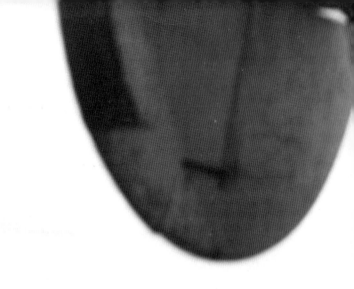

B-17G-70-DL 44-6915 of the 524th BS, 379th BG, which failed to return on 19 March 1945 when Lt James Poynor was forced to land the aircraft at Brussels, Belgium while returning from a mission. The B-17 was eventually returned to the USA via England and was scrapped in the same year. (USAF)

INTRODUCTION

The 8th Air Force was constituted as VIIIth Bomber Command on 19 January 1942 and activated at Savannah AAB, Georgia, on 28 January 1942. On 23 February Major General Ira C. Eaker was appointed VIIIth BC Commander. The appointment of Maj Gen. Carl A. Spaatz as the Commanding General of the 8th AF was announced on 2 May. Four B-17E/F Flying Fortress groups - the 92nd, 97th, 301st and 303rd (and two B-24D Liberator groups) formed the nucleus of the heavy bombardment force in England. First to arrive in the UK was the ground echelon of the 97th BG, which disembarked on 9 June and entrained for its Polebrook base in Northamptonshire; from where RAF Fortress Is had once flown raids over Germany.

It took time to get the new groups ready for combat, and training was lacking in many areas. The first Fortress strike of the war went ahead on 17 August 1942, when the 97th BG attacked the marshalling yards at Rouen Sotteville in north-west France. Eaker's ability to wage a bombing offensive was hampered by the more pressing needs of Brig-Gen James H. Doolittle's 12th AF, which would have to be equipped and trained to support the *Torch* invasion of North-west Africa in November 1942. The 8th AF was thus denied valuable replacement men and machines and Eaker sent all he had on missions to attack shipyards and airfields on the Continent. On 14 September both the 97th and 301st BGs were assigned to the 12th Air Force. The 97th flew their 14th and last 8th AF mission on 21 October 1942. The 301st BG flew their eighth and last mission in the 8th AF on 8 November 1942.

The offensive against U-boat bases and construction yards began in October 1942, and it remained the main focus of the 8th AF until June 1943. In the course of this campaign, 2,500 tons of bombs were dropped on enemy targets. Early raids by heavy bombers (mostly B-17s) from England in 1942 were flown at altitudes of around 20,000-25,000 ft. Even at these altitudes bombers were relatively easy targets for the flak crews and fighter attacks by the Luftwaffe. On almost every mission bombers were hitting the target, but not in large enough concentrations to cause serious damage. Experience proved that a single bomb, or even a few bombs, did not have enough destructive power on their own.

Col (later General) Curtis E. LeMay, CO of the 305th BG was determined to achieve greater bombing accuracy by flying a straight course on the bomb run instead of zigzagging every ten seconds - a tactic, which had been designed to spoil the aim of the German flak batteries. His plan was to cross the target faster, and therefore reduce the amount of time available to the German flak batteries to fire on the formation. At Chelveston, LeMay worked hard to find the best method of combating fighter attacks without compromising bombing accuracy, and vice versa. He was a great believer in 'close group formations': aircraft flying quite close together, changing the wingmen of all three squadrons up or down depending on the direction of attack by enemy fighters. LeMay wanted the group to fly as closely as possible without compromising safety and to be able to shift the formation to direct as much firepower at the enemy fighter as possible. After trying 'stacked-up' formations of eighteen aircraft, LeMay finally decided upon staggered three-plane elements within squadrons and staggered squadrons within groups. This would result in a complicated bombing procedure if each aircraft tried manoeuvering to enable accurate aiming, so LeMay discarded individual bombing, which had been standard operating procedure from the outset. He replaced the technique with 'lead crews', whose bombardier signalled to the rest of the formation when to bomb, so that all bombs were released simultaneously no matter what formation the aircraft were flying. This simple but brilliant idea could lead to all the bombs missing the target, but if they all landed a short distance from the mean point of impact, then a target could be successfully destroyed instead of damaged. The very best bombardiers were selected for the task and put into lead crews. On 18 March 1943 the 305th BG, flying at 24,000 ft, placed 76 per cent of its bomb load within 1,000 ft of the MPI at

Vegesack. It was on this mission that automatic flight control equipment was used in combat for the first time. LeMay's tactics found support at Wing Headquarters, and gradually lead crews, comprising highly trained pilots, bombardiers and navigators, became standard operating procedure.

The primary object of the joint US/British bomber offensive in 1943 was, '*The progressive destruction and dislocation of the German military, industrial and economic system, and the undermining of the morale of the German people to a point where their capacity for armed resistance is fatally weakened.*' The intermediate objective was German fighter strength, but the primary objectives were German submarine yards and bases, the remainder of the German aircraft industry, ball-bearing factories and oil facilities. The secondary objectives were synthetic rubber and tyre production facilities and military motor transport vehicles. The *Pointblank* Directive of 18 May 1943 set the pattern for the rest of the war, with the USAAF bombing by day and the RAF Bomber Command by night in a round-the-clock bomber offensive. On 13 February 1944 *Pointblank* was modified to give first priority to the destruction of the German single-engine and twin-engine air frame and component production; and Axis-controlled ball-bearing production. Second priority was Installations supporting the German Air Force.

Below: **B-17G-15-DL 42-37853/E** *Leading Lady,* **which was assigned to the 452nd BG in October 1943 and in 1944 was transferred to the 388th BG at Knettishall. This aircraft and Lt Campbell's crew crash-landed at Eastchurch on 4 January 1944 returning from the mission to Munster and the B-17 was later salvaged. (Ab Jansen via Theo Boiten) (USAF)**

THE B-17 GROUP AND FORMATION PROCEDURES

Each group consisted of four squadrons of approximately twelve aircraft, based on one airfield. Squadrons were further divided, for purposes of flight control, into flights (six aircraft) and elements (three aircraft). On missions, 8th AF bomb groups took off and assembled into squadrons, then groups, and then wings. 'Combat boxes' assembled in the vicinity of the airfield, 'combat wings' assembled at a place, time and altitude prescribed by the combat wing commander, normally with the leader at 2,500 ft, in a column of combat boxes, each combat box in staggered formation. The following combat boxes took position slightly above the lead combat box and flew in close formation in column. Each combat wing was assigned an area in which to form the combat boxes into combat wing formation. Each combat wing consisted of two or three combat boxes. When more than four combat boxes were employed, they would not normally attempt to close up into single formation, but would form two or more combat wings.

Above: **Formation flying was tiring for the pilots but essential for defence and bombing accuracy. Sadly, collisions were inevitable such as the one below when, on 22 October 1944, two Fortresses of the 305th BG, returning from a mission to Hannover, collided at 1710 hrs over the 306th BG base at Thurleigh. Seventeen airmen were killed in this accident; there were no survivors.**
(T/Sgt Francis L. Waugh USAF)

In April 1943 four new B-17F groups arrived in England. A fifth 'new' B-17 group was added to the force when the 92nd BG resumed bombing operations. Around this time the unit designations were changed from 'combat boxes' and 'combat groups' to 'groups' and 'wings'. The term 'combat wing' remained in use to describe the battle formation composed of two or three group boxes. A wing would normally assemble on a line about 30-40 miles long, with time and altitude prescribed for the lead combat

Above: B-17F-100-BO 42-30362 *Wee Bonnie II* of the 561st BS dropping its bombs on target. (USAF)

wing at each end of the 'assembly line'. The assembly line was normally chosen at an angle to the first leg of the route, in order to permit the lead navigator to establish his ground speed and drift, to determine the strength and direction of the wind, while still over land, and to permit following combat wings to cut across in order to catch up, if they were late. Whenever possible, the ends of the wing assembly line were chosen to coincide with 'Splasher' radio beacon sites or MF/DF beacon sites, so that the radio compasses could be used to aid in assembly in overcast or broken overcast conditions when geographical landmarks might be obscured.

In June 1943 the 94th, 95th and 96th BGs formed a new 4th Bomb Wing in Essex and Suffolk under the command of Brig.-Gen. Fred L. Anderson. Following high losses, the 8th AF Marauder groups were transferred from the 3rd Bomb Wing to VIII Air Support Command and their Essex bases were taken over by three B-17 groups in the 4th Wing, while the arrival of the 100th, 385th and 388th Groups, would increase the 4th Wing to six groups. The new 4th Wing CO, Col. Curtis E. LeMay, moved into the former 3rd Wing HQ at Elveden Hall, near Thetford. By September 1943 VIII Bomber Command totalled nine B-17 groups (1st Bomb Wing) and four B-24 groups (2nd Bomb Wing).

The organizational structure described above remained in existence until 13 September 1943, when VIII Bomber Command was officially divided into three bombardment divisions (and from 1 January 1945 into air divisions). The heavy bomb groups lost their provisional combat bombardment wings, which became simply combat bombardment wings. Each division controlled three to five combat bombardment wings, and each combat bombardment wing comprised, generally, three groups. Each division in the 8th AF controlled several bombardment and fighter groups.

Sometimes all divisions would attack the same target or group of targets in a given area, but quite often the targets assigned on any one day differed according to the make-up of the division. The main reason for this was because the 3rd (until its changeover to an all-B-17 force) and 2nd Bomb Divisions operated Liberators, which were faster and had different power settings to the B-17s. Gen. James Doolittle did try to convert the 8th AF to an all-B-17 force, but not enough Fortresses were available.

8th AF B-17 TIMELINE

1942

23 February   8th AF arrives in England.

23 April   Brig.-Gen. Ira C. Eaker appointed Chief, VIII Bomber Command in Europe.

17 August   First US heavy bomber raid against railyards at Rouen, France, by B-17s of the 97th BG.

20 October   Brig.-Gen. Asa N. Duncan, Chief of Air Staff, issues a revised set of objectives to be carried out by VIII BC. In part, it states: *'Until further orders every effort of the VIII Bomber Command will be directed to obtaining the maximum destruction of the submarine bases in the Bay of Biscay.'* The limited number of Fortresses available prevents VIII Bomber Command hitting submarine yards inside Germany.

1943

23 January   Casablanca Conference. Ira C. Eaker, acting Commanding General, 8th AF, wins his case for continued daylight bombing. Marks the start of the Combined Bomber offensive in Europe by the USAAF by day and RAF Bomber Command by night, otherwise known as 'round the clock' bombing.

27 January   To demonstrate that daylight precision bombing can triumph over area bombing by night, Eaker orders first US attack on Germany (U-boat construction yards at Wilhelmshaven); 91 B-17s and B-24s despatched, but bad weather reduces the attacking force to 53 B-l7s, which drop their bombs on the shipyards from 25,000 ft through a German smoke screen (2 others bomb Emden). Despite heavy fighter opposition, only three bombers shot down.

June   *Operation Pointblank*, an intermediate priority objective aimed at the German fighter strength, is finally published. Primary objectives listed are the *'German submarine yards and bases, the remainder of the German aircraft industry, ball bearings and oil'*; secondary objectives: *'synthetic rubber and tyres and military motor transport vehicles'*. The CBO plan calls for 2,702 heavy bombers in 51 groups to be in place before the Allied invasion, planned for mid-1944.

22 June   First really deep penetration of Germany, to the synthetic rubber plant at Huls, Germany. 235 B-17s despatched; most of the route is flown without escort. 16 B-17s are lost and 170 damaged; 183 Fortresses bomb plant so effectively that full production is not resumed for six months.

17 July   Record 322 8th AF bombers despatched to Hanover.

24 July   *'Blitz Week'* begins with an attack by 324 B-17s of the 8th AF on targets in Norway, with one force flying a 2,000 mile round trip to Bergen and Trondheim, the longest US mission in Europe thus far. *'Blitz Week'* costs the 8th AF about 100 aircraft and 90 combat crews, which leaves fewer than 200 heavy bombers ready for combat.

15 August   *Starkey* deception plan created to make Germany believe that an invasion of the French coast is imminent.

17 August   376 8th AF B-17s bomb the Schweinfurt ball bearing plant and the aircraft plants at Regensburg. 60 B-17s are shot down - 36 at Schweinfurt and 24 at Regensburg. 27 B-17s are so badly damaged they never fly again; 60 B-17s of the 4th Wing, which continue to North Africa have to be left there for repair.

9 September   Precision bombing of Fw 190 plant at Marienburg, Germany, by 96 B-17s of the 8th AF with 60 per cent of all bombs dropped exploding within 1,000 ft of the MPI and 83 per cent within 2,000 ft.

14 October   Second Schweinfurt raid: 291 B-17s attack, 60 aircraft lost, and damage sustained to 138 B- 17s that return to England.

1944

1 January   US Strategic Air Forces in Europe Command established to control operations of 8th and 15th AFs.

19-26 February '*Big Week*' series of sustained raids on German aircraft industry. Total losses amount to 226 US bombers.

4-6 March   B-17s of the 8th AF bomb Kleinmachnow area, southwest of Berlin, becoming the first US bombers to attack the German capital. On 6 March, 730 heavy bombers and almost 800 escort fighters are despatched by 8th AF to Berlin.

March-June   Interdiction campaign to isolate northwestern France, the area of *Operation Overlord*.

19 Mar-11 May   *Operation Strangle*: interdiction campaign to choke off German rail supply in Italy.

6 June   *Operation Overlord*, the invasion of northwest France: 8,722 AAF aircraft over France in support of the operation. Altogether, 2,362 bomber sorties involving 1,729 B-17s and B-24s are flown on D-Day, dropping 3,596 tons of bombs.

21 June   Second *Frantic* shuttle mission, by 8th AF B-17s, escorted by 61 P-5ls, who bomb a synthetic oil refinery just south of Berlin and then fly on to landing fields in the Ukraine, 144 B-17s land in the Ukraine; 73 at Poltava, remainder at Mirgorod. German raid on Poltava, 21/22 June, destroys 47 B-17s and damages 29 others.   26 June, 72 Fortresses fly home, bombing a target in Poland and staging through Italy, then bombing a target in France en route to England on 5 July. Entire tour covers 6,000 miles, ten countries and 29% hours of operational flying.

14 July   *Operation Cadillac*: mass drop by 322 8th AF B-17s of 3,780 supply containers to the French Forces of the Interior (FFI).

6 August   76 Fortresses in the 95th and 390th Bomb Group, 8th AF, and 64 P-51s fly shuttle mission to Russia, bombing the Focke Wulf plant at Rahmel, Poland, en route. They fly a raid to the Trzebinia synthetic oil refinery and return to Russia before flying to Italy, 8 August, bombing two Romanian airfields en route. 12 August they fly back to Britain on the last stage of their shuttle, bombing a French airfield en route.

11 September   Final *Frantic* mission: 75 B-17s and 64 P-51s of the 8th AF attacks Chemnitz and fly on to the Soviet Union. 13 September the B-17s bomb steel works at Diosgy^r, Hungary, and land in Italy.

18 September   117 B-17s of the 8th AF drop 1,284 containers of ammunition, guns and supplies to Poles in beleaguered Warsaw, but only 130 fall into the right hands.

1945

January   US tactical air forces help defeat German forces engaged in the '*Battle of the Bulge*', the last enemy offensive in the west.

13-15 February 8th AF and RAF Bomber Command raze German city of Dresden. HE and firestorms cause 35,000 civilian deaths.

7 May   German representatives surrender in the west. War in Europe ends. VE Day proclaimed on 8 May 1945. Russians accept surrender, 9 May.

THE GROUPS

34TH
BOMB GROUP

34th Bombardment Group (H)
3rd BD

Component Squadrons
4th, 7th, 18th and 391st Bombardment Squadrons (H)
Operated the B-17
17 September 1944
-
20 April 1945
Wartime Base
Mendlesham
Total Missions
170 (62 B-24)
Total Bomb Tonnage
13,424.6 tons
(131.6 tons leaflets, etc)
Aircraft MIA
34
Other Op. Losses: 39
Claims to Fame
Lost no bombers to enemy fighter action over enemy territory. Only losses to enemy aircraft over own base.

Oldest USAAF bomb group to serve in 8th AF.

Above: B-17Gs of the group flying through flak. Top aircraft is 43-38286/T Flying Dutchman of the 7th BS, which was scrapped at Kingman, Arizona in late 1945. (USAF)

Below: Natural metal finish B-17Gs of the Mendlesham group in formation. (USAF)

Above: **Natural metal finish B-17Gs of the 391st BS, in formation amid flak bursts in 1944. (USAF)**

Below: B-17G-80-VE 44-8731 *Knockout Dropper* was assigned to the 332nd BS, 94th BG at Rougham on 24 January 1944 and was transferred to the 34th BG at Mendlesham where it was allocated to the 4th BS on 26 January 1945. It is pictured here with the green nose-band of the 391st BS. *Knockout Dropper* returned to the ZOI and was broken up for scrap at Walnut Ridge late in 1945. (USAF)

91ST

BOMB GROUP

91st Bombardment Group (H)
'The Ragged Irregulars'
1ST BD

Component Squadrons
322nd, 323rd, 324th and 401st Bombardment Squadrons (H)

Operated the B-17
7 Nov. 42 - 25 Apr. 45

Wartime Bases
Kimbolton
Bassingbourn

Total Missions
340

Total Bomb Tonnage
22,142.3 tons

Aircraft MIA
197

Claims to Fame
Two Distinguished Unit Citations;
11 Jan. 44 - Oschersleben
4 Mar. 43 - Hamm

Highest total claims of e/a destroyed of all 8th AF bomb groups (420).

Highest losses of all 8th AF bomb groups.

First group to attack a target in the Ruhr (4 Mar 43 Hamm).

Led the famous Schweinfurt mission of 17 Aug 43.

First 8th AF bomb group to complete 100 Missions (5 Jan 44).

Selected to test first flak suits (Mar. 43).

B-17G *Nine-O-Nine* completed 140 missions without an abort; an 8th AF record.

Right: B-17F-15-BO 41-24490 *Jack the Ripper* of the 324th BS went missing in action on 22 February 1944 with the loss of 1/Lt James I. Considine's crew. *See facing page.* (USAF)

Above: B-17F-20-BO 41-24524 *The Eagle's Wrath* of the 323rd BS and Lt Anthony G. Arcaro's crew FTR on the 17 August 1943 mission to Schweinfurt. (USAF)

Below: B-17F-10-VE 42-5729 *Buccaneer* of the 401st BS taking off from Bassingbourn. This B-17F first served as *The Piccadilly Commando* in the 369th BS, 306th BG from 18 February - 7 September 1943. *Buccaneer* was returned to the USA in March 1944 (USAF)

Above: B-17F-75-BO 42-29837 *Lady Luck* and B-17F-15-BO 41-24490 *Jack the Ripper* of the 324th BS, over France en route to their target at Tours on 5 January 1944. *Jack the Ripper* became the last of the original B-17Fs assigned to the 91st BG to be shot down, being lost on a raid on Bunde near Osnabruck on 22 February 1944. *Lady Luck* joined AFSC on 6 April 1944 and then transferred to the MTO where it operated in Italy before returning to the US in June 1944. She was scrapped in July 1945. (USAF)

Right: Capt Robert K Morgan and the crew of B-17F-10-BO 41-24485 *"MEMPHIS BELLE"* of the 324th BS bid farewell to Generals Devers and Eaker at Bassingbourn on 13 June 1943 before flying home to begin a Bond Tour of the USA. The crew flew their 25th, and final, mission of their tour on 17 May 1943 to Lorient. The *'BELLE* featured in a 1943 documentary about Eighth Air Force operations, made principally for American cinema audiences by Maj William Wyler, the famous Hollywood director (USAF)

Above: A Messerschmitt Bf110 attacks a formation of 91st BG B-17s approaching their target on 22 January 1944. (USAF)

Left: B-17F-15-VE 42-5763 *Bomb-Boogie* of the 401st BS. On 6 September 1943 this Fortress, flown by I/Lt Elwood D Arp's crew, was one of 45 'heavies' shot down on the mission to the aircraft components factories at Stuttgart. (USAF)

Below: B-17F-25-DL 42-3111 *Local Girl* of the 324th BS, which came under Bf109 attack and exploded over Geefsweer village in Groningen Province returning from a raid on Emden on 27 September 1943. 2/Lt William G. Peagram, pilot, remained at the controls while eight crew bailed out over the coast of Ems. Peagram and Melvin Peters, waist gunner, who went on firing to the end, were found dead in the wreckage. Larson, engineer, and Cosgrove, navigator, drowned when the cords of their parachutes became entangled in the *"botschuttings"* or "flounder fences"; a device of twigs and branches to catch flat fish. Norman Eatinger, bombardier, was rescued by a Dutch fishing boat (via Orlo Natvig)

Right: B-17G-50-BO 42-102490 *Wicked Witch* was assigned to the 323rd BS on 22 April 1944. On its 70th mission on 20 February 1945 whilst being flown by 1/Lt Eddie R. McKnight's crew, it suffered a direct flak burst over Nurnberg, Germany. The pilots' compartment was hit and an explosion was observed, with fire coming from the right side. A flash was also seen emanating from the bomb bay. The aircraft was last spotted at 10.000 ft. approximately 25 km south of Nürnburg/Fürth. McKnight and five of his crew were killed in action, with the remaining three being made PoW. (via Robert M Foose)

Right: Crew of B-17F-65-BO 42-29679 *Ramblin' Wreck* in the 401st BS. L-R, back row: 1/Lt Don 'Pop' Shea, navigator; 2/Lt Clyde C. McCallum, co-pilot; 1/Lt William F Gibbons, pilot; Wendy Q. Baum, bombardier. Front row: T/Sgt William O. 'Blimp' Doupance, radio operator; S/Sgt Julius W. Edwards, left waist gunner; Bob Ginsburg, waist gunner; Sift Sgt Paul M. Goecke, tail gunner; Sgt Clarence R. 'Junior' Bateman, ball turret T/Sgt John R. Parsons, engineer top turret gunner. On 21 February 1944, this crew except Baum and Ginsburg were shot down by fighters in B-17F-20-DL 42-3073 *Lightning Strikes*. (via Walter A. Truax)

Right: Hollywood movie star Major Clark Gable poses with Lt George Birdsong's crew of B-17F-30-BO 42-5077 *Delta Rebel No 2* of the 323rd BS, while shooting sequences for the documentary Combat America. *Delta Rebel No.2* and 2/Lt Robert W. Thompson's crew FTR on 12 August 1943 when it crashed to earth at Bruninshausen killing four crew. Six men were taken into captivity. (USAF)

Above: B-17G-15-BO 42-31367 *Chow Hound* of the 322nd BS was issued to 1/Lt Jerold Newquist and crew, who decided on its unique nickname because they liked to 'fight to eat and eat to fight'. Tony Starcer painted a 'Pluto'-like cartoon hound riding a bomb on the nose of the B-17. *Chow Hound* flew its first mission on 29 January and Newquist completed 22 of his 25 combat missions in this aircraft. Lt Maynard Frey's crew added another 13 missions to its tally, including one on D-Day. 1/Lt Jack Thompson's crew then flew a further 13 missions in the bomber until it fell victim to a direct flak hit on 8 August when en route Caen, France a shell penetrated the centre fuselage before exploding, breaking the B-17 in two. None of the crew survived. (USAF)

Below: B-17G-35-DL 42-107027 *Hlikin' for Home* of the 322nd BS on a practice mission on 18 June 1944. (USAF via Mike Bailey)

Below: B-17G-30-BO 42-31909 *Nine-O-Nine* (named after the last three digits of its serial number) which was assigned to the 323rd BS in February 1944 and which completed over 125 missions without a turnback. This photo was taken on 18 June 1945 when this famous Fortress had completed no less than 140 missions. It stands with other '*war wearies*' waiting to be scrapped. (USAF)

Right and below right: **Having lost three engines over the target at Osnabruck on the 22 December 1943 mission, B-17F-30-DL 42-3184 PY-Q** *USS Aliquippa*, **407th BS, 92nd BG struggled westward on one engine before finally coming down near Azelo, Bornerbroek, eastern Holland. Lt Gene Wiley's crew and Gen Delmar T Spivey were taken prisoner.** (Coen Cornelissen)

Below: B-17E 41-9020 *Phyllis* was assigned to the 340th BS, 97th BG at Polebrook in March 1942 before joining the 92nd BG at Bovingdon in August..

Bottom: B-17F-1-BO 41-24341 was modified as an escort aircraft by Vega and became known as the XB-40 (pictured at Burbank on the occasion of its first flight, 10 November 1942). XB-40s made their operational debut on 29 May 1943, when seven in the 92nd BG took part on a mission for the first time. Losses were not made good, although the YB-40s continued flying missions until the end of July 1943. (Boeing)

92nd

BOMB GROUP

92nd Bombardment Group (H)
'Fame's Favoured Few'
1ST BD

Component Squadrons
325th, 326th, 327th and 407th Bombardment Squadron (H)
Operated the B-17
August 1942 - May 1945
Wartime Bases
Bovingdon, Alconbury, Podington
Total Missions
308
Total Bomb Tonnage
20,829.4 tons
Aircraft MIA
154
Claims to Fame
Distinguished Unit Citation 11 Jan.44

Medal of Honor: Flight Officer John C. Morgan, 26 Jul. 43: Hanover.

Oldest Group in 8th AF.

Group's 327th BS only unit in USAAF to be equipped with YB-40 for combat.

Flew the secret Disney rocket-bomb experimental missions early in 1945.

Acted as VIII BC Combat Crew Replacement Centre Aug 42-May 43.

Led 8th AF on last mission of war.

Above: B-17E 41-9019 *"Little Skunk Face"* of the 414th BS, 97th BG in early RAF-style camouflage. This aircraft transferred to the 305th BG on 6 November 1942 and was later used by the 381st BG in June 1943. The following month it went to the 327th BS, 92nd BG where it served as a target tug. On 27 August 1943 it made its last move within the front-line force, being passed on to the 482nd BG at Alconbury. 41-9019 was finally written off on 21 August 1945. (USAF)

Right: B-17F-70-DL 42-3494 of the 407th BS, which crashed at Podington on 6 September 1943 returning from a raid on Stuttgart. (Joseph Minton via Larry Goldstein)

Left: B-17E 41-9023 *Yankee Doodle* was first assigned to the 92nd BG at MacDill Field on 13 March 1942. On 11 May the aircraft was transferred to the 414th BS, 97th BG, and once in England it was one of 12 E-models that took part in the Eighth Air Force's first B-17 mission of the war, flown on 17 August 1942. Piloted by John Dowswell, it carried Brig Gen Ira C Eaker to Rouen. Seven days later, 41-9023 returned to the 92nd BG where it served until 31 March 1943, when it joined the Blind Approach Training Flight (BATF) at Bassingbourn. In August 41-9023 was transferred again, this time to the 322nd BS and it ended its ETO service with the 324th BS as a target tow and general liaison aircraft. (USAF)

94th

BOMB GROUP

94th Bombardment Group (H) 3RD BD

Component Squadrons
331st, 332nd, 333rd and 410th Bombardment Squadrons (H)
Operated the B-17
13 May 43
-
21 April 1945
Wartime Bases
Bassingbourn
Earls Colne, Bury St Edmunds (Rougham)
Total Missions
324
Total Bomb Tonnage
18,924.6 tons
(226.2 tons supplies, etc.)
Aircraft MIA
153
Other Op. Losses: 27
Claims to Fame
Two Distinguished Unit Citations:
17 Aug. 43: Regensburg
11 Jan. 44: Brunswick

Above left: **B-I7F-95-BO 42-30248** of the 410th BS, which took the name *The Southern Queen* in July 1943. In August this aircraft joined the 333rd Squadron and became *The Buzzard*, and was later renamed *Prodigal Son*, before finally becoming *Lassie Come Home*. Unfortunately she did not on 11 January 1944, failing to return with Lt Robert C. Randall's crew, two of whom were killed, and eight made prisoner. (via Geoff Ward)

Left: **B-17F-25-DL 42-3082** *Double Trouble* of the 333rd BS. The pilot, Lt Bill Winnesheik, aborted the mission to Bremen on 25 June 1943 after fighters knocked out two engines and he landed in England despite a full bomb load. On 4 October 1943, during a mission to St. Dizier, France, fighters knocked out the No 3 engine and the propeller refused to feather but the crew managed to crash-land at Margate and the bomber was duly salvaged. (USAF)

Left, A stick of 1,000 lb bombs dropped from Lt John Winslett's B-I7G-30-VE 42-97791 *Trudy* in the 332nd BS over Berlin on 19 May 1944 knocked off the left horizontal stabilizer of Lt Marion Ulysses Reid's B-17G-20-BO 42-31540 *Miss Donna Mae* in the 331st BS, below. Reid's aircraft went into an uncontrollable spin and at 13,000 ft the wing broke off and the B-17 spun crazily to the ground. There were no survivors. (USAF via Abe Dolim)

Right: B-1790-BO 42-30146 *Down and Go!* (formerly *Cherokee*), in the 333rd BS FTR with 2/Lt Ned Palmer's crew on 29 July 1943. One man was KIA and nine made PoW. The B-17 landed intact in France and was used by KG200, being serialled A3+CE 230146 ('2), here attracting a large crowd whilst visiting Parndorf airfield to the east of Vienna in the summer of 1944. (via Hans-Heri Stapfer)

Below and lower right: B-17F-35-DL 42-3190, of the 332nd BS in a French wheat field with its bomb load intact after being shot up on the Paris-Le Bourget mission of 14 July 1943 by Oberstleutnant Egon Mayer, *Kommandeur, III./JG2*. (The 94th BG lost four B-17s, the total losses for the Le Bourget strike). Captain Kee Harrison elected to crash-land the Fortress to save the engineer, whose parachute had been burned in the fire aboard the aircraft. Harrison, his co-pilot, and the engineer, managed to escape with the help of the French Underground. They walked across the Pyrenees into Spain. Four others were made PoW (via Harry Holmes)

Above: B-17F-50-DL 42-3352 *Virgin's Delight* piloted by Lt R. E 'Dick' LePore of the 410th lead squadron, photographed by Captain Ray D. Miller, the 410th BS Flight Surgeon leaving the burning Fw 190 factory at Marienburg on 9 October 1943. On the bomb run Le Pore was not using oxygen, and was in fact eating a Mars' bar from his PX rations! The target was completely demolished. Anti-aircraft defences were thought unnecessary to defend a target so far from England, which allowed the heavies to bomb from 11,000-13,000 ft. At these heights accuracy was almost guaranteed: 60 per cent of the bombs dropped by the 96 Fortresses exploded within 1,000 ft of the MPI, and 83 per cent fell within 2,000 ft. Before the raid the Marienburg plant had been turning out almost 50 per cent of the *Luftwaffe's* Fw 190 production. General Eaker called it a '*classic example of precision bombing'. Virgin's Delight* and 2/Lt Walter Chyle's crew failed to return on 29 November 1943, when the aircraft was ditched in the North Sea with the loss of all the crew. (USAF)

Above right: All eight crewmembers in Maj. Lewis Gordon Thorup's crew of B-17F-65-BO 42-29708 *Shackeroo!* of the 333rd BS, who were rescued by MTB 245 after ditching in the North Sea after a German fighter attack during the mission to Kiel on 13 June 1943. It was one of nine Fortresses of the 94th BG lost on this raid. CO of this 22nd MTB Flotilla boat was Lt Douglas Hunt RNVR (second from left). Col Thorup commanded the 447th BG. from 31 March-30 June 1945. (Douglas Hunt DSC*via Theo Boiten)

Right: On 25 July 1943, Lt John P Keelan and crew of B-17F-90-BO 42-30206 *Happy Daze*, 410th BS ditched in the North Sea returning from the raid on Kiel. One crewmember was KIA but on 26 July an airborne lifeboat was dropped by a 279 Squadron RAF Warwick from Bircham Newton near to the ditched crew and the other nine men returned safely to England. (Dick Vimpany)

Right: Boulton Paul Defiant TT1 DR945, one of two loaned to the 8th AF at Bovingdon in 1942 and operated over the gunnery school at Snettisham, Norfolk in 1943. It was passed to the 94th BG at Bury St Edmunds for some months, where this photo is thought to have been taken, before being returned to the RAF in August 1944.
(H. Freidman collection via GMS)

Below: B-17F-65-BO 42-29670 *"Thundermug"* of the 333rd BS was transferred to the 544th BS, 384th BG. It was one of seven in the Group that were lost on 25 July 1943 when it went MIA with Lt Kelmer J Hall's crew. Two men were KIA, eight were PoW after the B-17 crashed at Hamburg. (Richards)

Below right: Master Sergeant Hugh K. Crawford, the crew chief, attends to an engine on B-17G-45-BO 42-97358 *Ordnance Express* of the 332nd BS at Rougham in December 1944. *Ordnance Express* survived the war and ended up as scrap at Kingman, Arizona in late 1945. (Crawford)

Below: Armament ground crews take out the machine guns from the turrets of B-17G-95-BO 43-38834 *Tutorwolf* of the 332nd BS following a mission late in 1944. *Tutorwolf* was scrapped in December 1945 at Kingman, Arizona.
(via Abe Dolim)

Above: B-17F-90-BO 42-30173 *Circe* of the 412th BS completed its first operational sortie on 22 June 1943. It was lost whilst being flown by Lt James D Pearson's crew on the 10 February 1944 mission to Brunswick, the aircraft dropping out of formation on fire near Lingen. Three crew died, while seven, including Pearson, were made PoWs. (USAF via Mike Bailey)

Left: B-17G-80-VE 44-8782 of the 412th BS with *H2X* radome extended. This aircraft flew its first sortie on 25 February 1945 and was assigned to the 100th BG on 25 May 1945 before being scrapped at Walnut Ridge, Arkansas, in 1946. (USAF)

Below: B-17F-30-DL 42-3153 *The Devil's Daughter* of the 336th BS flown by Lt R. E. Fischer's crew, drops its bombs over the target Wilhelmshaven on 3 November 1943. (USAF via Mike Bailey)

95th Bombardment Group (H) 3RD BD

Component Squadrons
334th, 335th, 336th and 412th Bombardment Squadrons (H)
Operated the B-17
13 May 1943
-
20 April 1945
Wartime Bases
Alconbury, Framlingham, Horham
Total Missions
320
(6 food missions May 1945)
Total Bomb Tonnage
19,769.2 tons
(211 tons supplies, etc.)
Aircraft MIA
157
Other Op. Losses: 39
Claims to Fame
Only 8th AF group awarded three Distinguished Unit Citations;
17 Aug. 43 Regensburg
10 Oct 43 Munster
4 Mar 44 Berlin

First USAAF group to bomb Berlin (4 Mar 44)

Last a/c lost by 8th AF on a mission, 7 May 45.

First 8th AF general KIA while flying with this group (13 Jun. 43)

Top left: A 95th BG B-17G approaches the 486th BG base at Sudbury (Acton) in Suffolk. (USAF)

Top right: On 7 May 1945 the Eighth Air Force flew its sixth, and final, *Chowhound* mission to Holland. Two Fortresses had already been lost earlier in the operation when they collided soon after take-off, and on the 7th the supply drops claimed a third victim, B-17G-75-VE 44-8640 of the 334th BS. A veteran of 58 bombing missions and six food drops, it was lost over the North Sea with Lt Lionel N. 'Spider' Sceurman's crew of eight and six passengers from the Horham photographic section, after their food drop near Hilversum. Co-pilot Lt James R Schwarz and toggelier S/Sgt David C Condon, were picked up by an air-sea rescue crew in an OA-1OA Catalina of the 5th ERS at Halesworth. Navigator Lt Russell J Cook was also rescued, by an RAF Walrus, but died before reaching hospital. No one else survived. 44-8640 was the last Eighth Air Force aircraft lost in World War 2 (via the late Ken Wright)

Left: B-17G-15-DL 42-37889 *Pride of Chehalis*, 336th BS, being inspected by locals after crashing in a potato field near Vroomshoop, the Netherlands on 29 June 1944, when 1,150 B-17s and B-24s were despatched to bomb the synthetic oil plant at Böhlen, a ball bearing works and 11 aircraft assembly plants in the Leipzig area. 1/Lt J. D. Cook and his crew bailed out safely before the Fortress, one of 15 bombers lost, went down. Two men evaded capture. A total of 391 heavies returned with battle damage. (Coen Cornelissen)

Below: B-17G-10-BO 42-31329 of the 334th BS, which crash-landed at Oberriet-Kriessern, Switzerland, on the mission to Augsburg, 16 March 1944. Five of Lt James W. Reed's crew were interned and five were made PoW. (via Hans Heiri Stapfer)

96th Bombardment Group (H)
'Snetterton Falcons'
3rd BD

Component Squadrons
337th, 338th, 339th and 413th Bombardment Squadron (H)
Operated the B-17
14 May 1943
-
21 April 1945
Wartime Bases
Grafton Underwood, Andrews Field, Snetterton Heath
Total Missions
321
Total Bomb Tonnage
19,277.3 tons.
(131.6 tons supplies, etc.)
Aircraft MIA
189
Other Op. Losses: 50
Claims to Fame
Two Distinguished Unit Citations;
17 Aug. 43 Regensburg
9 Apr. 44 Poznan

Second highest MIA losses in 8th AF and highest in 3rd BD.

Highest loss rate sustained by any 8th AF group (first five months 1944).

Led mission Regensburg-Africa 17 Aug. 43

Above: B-17G-1-BO 42-31053 *Stingy*, was assigned to the 338th BS on 29 September 1943. Although said to have been named by Maj Gen Frederick L Anderson, Deputy CO of Operations USSTAF in honour of his son, one crew who flew it regularly called themselves the *'flying misers'*. On a training flight on 11 October 1944 *Stingy*, flown by Lt Nickolas Jorgenson, was involved in a mid-air collision when the pilot of B-17F-75-DL 42-3510 pulled up and hit the nose of B-17G-70-BO 43-37684 with its tail section. Just as '510 sheared in half, *Stingy* hit '684 with its rudder and also broke in two. Lt Jack C Core, piloting '510 parachuted to safety, while his B-17 and *Stingy* crashed at Woodend, west of Towcester. Core's four crew were killed, as was Jorgenson and his six-man crew. Although badly damaged, 43-37684 was able to limp back to Snetterton. (via Geoff Ward)

Below: B-17G-40-BO 42-97167 of the 339th BS with Capt Jack E Link's crew was shot down by fighters near Hahnsatten, Germany on 12 May 1944. Nine of the crew were killed and one made a PoW. When this photograph was taken, the ill-fated bomber had only been partially stripped of its Olive Drab paint (USAF)

DOUBLE STRIKE AUGUST 17 1943

On 17 August, the anniversary mission of the 8th AF the Fortresses attacked aircraft plants at Schweinfurt and Regensburg simultaneously. The Luftwaffe's operational fighter strength on the western front was showing a significant increase and Regensburg was the second largest aircraft plant of its kind in Europe, the largest being at Wiener Neustadt near Vienna. Production at Regensburg was estimated at 200 Me 109s a month, or approximately 25-30 per cent of Germany's single engine aircraft production. Brig- Gen Robert Williams, CO, 1st BW led his force to Schweinfurt while Col Curtis E. LeMay led the 4th BW to Regensburg. To minimise attacks from enemy fighters Le May's B-17s flew on to North Africa after the target. The 1st BW, meanwhile, flew a parallel course to Schweinfurt to further confuse the enemy defences and return to England after the raid. Altogether, the 4th BW lost 24 bombers, with the 100th Bomb Group's nine losses the highest loss of all. Attacks on the Schweinfurt force cost 36 Fortresses. Worst hit B-17 groups were the 381st and 91st, which lost eleven and ten B-17s respectively. Twenty-seven B-17s in the 1st BW were so badly damaged that they never flew again. Altogether, sixty B-17s were MIA (almost three times as high as the previous highest, on 13 June, when 26 bombers were lost). A further sixty Fortresses had to be left in North Africa pending repairs, so in the final analysis, 147 Fortresses had been lost to all causes on 17 August.

Above left: A 339th BS crew leave B-17F-100-BO 42-30359 after arriving in North Africa after the Regensburg mission of 17 August 1943. (via Geoff Ward)

Left: B-17F-95-BO 42-30325 *Miss Carry* of the 570th BS over the Alps on its way to North Africa on 17 August 1943. *Miss Carry* was involved in a mid-air collision with B-17F-100-BO 42-30334 *Virgin Sturgeon* near Hamelin, Germany, on 29 January 1944. The crew of the latter bomber, led by Lt William J Harding, was captured but Miss Carry returned safely to Framlingham. (via Ian McLachlan)

Below: B-17F-100-80 42-30372 *Shack Rabbit III* and B-17F-85-BO 42-30130 *Bubble Trouble* (later *The Klap-Trap 1I*, both from the 413th BS. cross the Brenner Pass, on the Austrian-Italian border, after the raid on Regensburg on 17 August 1943. 4th BW CO Col Curtis E. LeMay led the raid, flying with Capt Tom Kenney and his crew in B-17F-100-80 42-30366 *Fertile Myrtle III* in the 338th BS. This aircraft was badly shot up over Bremen on 16 December 1943 and crashed near Norwich after being abandoned over Norfolk by Kenney's crew. *Shack Rabbit III* was shot down by enemy fighters during the mission to Duren on 10 October 1943, four of its crew being killed, four captured and two evading. 42-30130 fell victim to flak on the 7 January 1944 mission to Ludwigshafen, crashing near Thionville, in France. Only two crew survived this incident to be made PoWs (via Geoff Ward)

Right: Sweating it out at Snetterton. (IWM)

Below right: B17F-110-BO 42-30607 *Pat Hand* of the 337th BS flown by Lt Ken E Murphy, suffered a direct flak hit over Paris just after bombs-away during the raid on the Hispano-Suiza aero-engine assembly plant on 15 September 1943. Just one member of its 11-man crew survived to become a PoW (USAF)

Below far right: B-17G-90-BO 43-38576 of the 413th BS was destroyed in a fire at Snetterton after a training flight on 28 December 1944. Piloted by Lt Len Kramer, the bomber overtook Lt Ed Onisko's B-17G-100-BO 43-38930 which had just landed on the main runway. As he did so his left wing and propellers scythed through the vertical stabilizer and right wing of Onisko's bomber. Incredibly, both crews escaped unhurt. Kramer's aircraft was wrecked, but Onisko's was repaired. (via Geoff Ward)

Below: B-17G-1-BO 42-31118 *Lady Millicent II* of the 338th BS, which belly landed on the grass at Snetterton Heath on 8 January 1944 and was salvaged five days later. (Joseph Minton via Larry Goldstein)

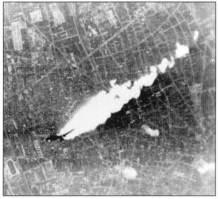

Left: B-17G-20-BO 42-31447 *Cookie* of the 338th BS was shot down by a German fighter over the Baltic during the mission to Rostock on 11 April 1944. All ten members of Lt Jack W Splan's crew were killed. The second Fortress in this photograph, B-17G-25-BO 42-31718 of the 337th BS, was also lost to enemy fighters, the bomber crashing at Hartmannshein, in Germany, on 12 May 1944 whilst on the mission to Zwickau. Two of 2/Lt Jerry T Musser's crew were killed and the remaining eight taken prisoner. (USAF)

Below: B-17F-90-BO 42-30188 *Temptation* (formerly *Kats Sass II*) of the 413th BS lost an engine on take-off on 4 February 1944 and Lt Joseph Meacham attempted a crash-landing at another as yet unfinished base nearby but the aircraft crashed short, in a field at East Shropham. All of Meacham's crew walked away from the wreckage. (via Robert E. Foose)

Left:B-17G-35-DL 42-107102 of the 413th BS suffered a mishap at Snetterton Heath on 19 January 1945 when the landing gear was retracted prematurely during a training flight. (Joseph Minton via Larry Goldstein)

Below: B-17G-70-BO 43-37716 *5 Grand* of the 338th BS, the 5,000th Boeing-built Fortress produced in Seattle since the attack on Pearl Harbor. Constructed in early 1944, the bomber had been christened by Mrs Gertrude Aldrich (a Boeing worker who had lost her son in a B-17) on 13 March that year by the breaking of the customary bottle of champagne against the chin turret. *5 Grand* was autographed by workers from the Boeing plant who scratched or wrote their names all over it. By the end of the war it had completed 78 missions, plus two food missions and two PoW trips. As the 96th BG were remaining in Germany as part of the army of occupation, the honour of returning *5 Grand* to the US went to Lt Thompson's crew of the 560th BS, 388th BG. Sadly *5 Grand* was cut up for scrap at the huge Kingman reclamation plant in Arizona before it could take its rightful place as a memorial in the city of Seattle. (USAF)

Above: *H2X*-equipped B-17G-60-VE 44-8399 which was assigned to the 337th BS on 5 January 1945 and survived the war (via Mike Bailey)

Below: B-17s of the 338th BS dropping bombs. Left is B-17F-100-BO 42-30363/M *Ruth L III*. Right is B-17F 100-BO 42-30373/T *Lucky Lady III*, which was lost on 8 October 1943 with Lt Warren A. Jones' crew. Five men were KIA and six were made PoW. (USAF)

Above:B-17G-45-BO 42-97212 of the 339th BS piloted by 1/Lt Sherman Gillespie, seeks refuge at Malmo, Sweden, shadowed by a Swedish Air Force J9 fighter after being damaged by enemy fighters on the mission to Rostock on 11 April 1944. In all, nine B-17s landed in Sweden on this day, and Gillespie's was one of eleven lost to the 96th. One was shot down by a *Luftwaffe* intruder over Suffolk. (USAF)

Below: B-17F of the 96th BG flying through thick flak in 1943. (USAF)

Above: **Fortresses of the 96th BG releasing their bombs on the Focke Wulf factory at Bremen, 26 November 1943. Nearest aircraft is B-17F-45-VE 42-6099** Winnie C. **of the 339th BS, later re-named** Ruth L **and used by the 337th BS. This Fortress and 2/Lt Nathan L. Young's crew failed to return on 22 March 1944. Six men were KIA and four MIA. (USAF)**

Left: **An overhead view of a 96th BG B-17G en route to its target in late 1944. Note the aircraft's group letter marking on the right wing. (via Geoff Ward)**

Above: **The 96th Bomb Group contributed 14 aircraft to** *Operation Zebra*, **which was mounted on 25 June 1944 in order to drop supplies to the** *FFI (French Forces of the Interior)*. **Photographed from a third Fortress, B-17G-60-BO 42-102978 of the 413th BS (note the 388th BG 'Square H' on the upper right wing) and B-17G-70-BO 43-37775** *Oh! Hard Luck* **of the 339th BS are seen flying in close formation over the French countryside. Escorted by large formations of fighters, only two B-17s were lost during** *Zebra*, **and two others aborted with mechanical problems. Both bombers survived the war and were returned to the US in July 1945. Further large-scale drops were made in July, August and September 1944. (USAF)**

Right: **B-17G-70-DL 44-6888** *Sweet Chariot* **of the 339th BS flown by Lt Harry Loveless, was written off in this crash landing at Snetterton Heath on 11 May 1945. (via Robert M. Foose)**

Above: B-17G-45-DL 44-6142 *The Stork* was assigned to the 337th BS at Snetterton on 4 June 1944 and was eventually returned to the US in early July 1945. The bomber was sold for scrap four months later. (via Geoff Ward)

100th
BOMB GROUP

100th Bombardment Group (H)
'The Bloody Hundredth'
3rd BD

Component Squadrons
349th, 350th, 351st and 418th Bombardment Squadron (H)

Wartime Bases
Podington
Thorpe Abbotts

Operated the B-17
25 Jun. 43 - 20 Apr. 45

Total Missions:
306
(6 food missions May 1945)

Total Bomb Tonnage
19,257.1 tons
(137.8 tons supplies, etc.)

Aircraft MIA
177
Other Op. Losses: 52

Claims to Fame
Two Distinguished Unit Citations;
17 Aug. 43: Regensburg
4/6/8 March 44: Berlin

Very high losses throughout period of combat.

Right: 1/Lt Donald K. Oakes' B-17F-85-BO 42-30080 *High Life* of the 351st BS was the first Fortress to land in neutral Switzerland, on 17 August 1943 during the raid on Regensburg. A 20-mm shell exploded in the No 3 engine nacelle cutting the throttle cable and caused an oil leak. Oakes feathered the propeller, but was then advised by ball turret gunner S/Sgt Leslie D. Nadeau of another major oil leak in the No 2 engine. The aircraft could not keep formation, so a forced landing was made at Dubendorf, a military airfield near Zurich. The Swiss originally planned to restore the bomber to airworthiness, but several fully serviceable B-17Fs arrived in Switzerland just days after this machine and *High Life* was eventually dismantled and taken to Kloten for storage. It was scrapped there post-war. (via Hans-Heiri Stapfer)

Above: On 11 August 1944, B-17F-45-VE 42-6087 *Royal Flush* of the 418th BS was hit by flak between the No 3 engine and the fuselage during a raid on Villacoublay near Paris. Flying its 75th mission, the bomber spiralled down and crashed in a field near Mendon. Four of 2/Lt Alfred Aske Jr's crew, who were on their fifth mission, were killed, one of whom was reportedly machine-gunned by German soldiers on the ground. Three crewmen were taken prisoner. Radio operator Charles Nekvasil and co-pilot Charles Barber evaded capture and returned to England. (via Charles H. Nekvasil)

Above: **View of 'Bombs Away' from a B-17 almost underneath!** (USAF)

Right: **On 10 October 1943 the 13th Wing went to Münster. The 100th reeled under the incessant attacks and 11 aircraft were shot down before the target.** *Royal Flush*, **which was flown by Robert Rosenthal because his usual aircraft was under repair, lost two engines over Münster and a rocket shell tore through the right wing, leaving a large hole. Despite this, Rosenthal completed the bomb run and instigated a series of violent manoeuvres to throw the aim of the flak guns. It was a great relief when the white vapour trails of the Thunderbolt escort were seen directly ahead. There were few B-17s for the "Little Friends" to protect. It had been a black day for the 13th CBW, which had lost 25 of the 29 B-17s lost by the 3rd BD. Worst of all; the 100th had lost 12 bombers. This brought its total losses to 19 in three days.** (USAF)

Top left: Lt Robert Wolf's B-17F-85-BO 42-30061 *Wolf Pack* (bottom) and two other 100th BG B-17s head for North Africa on 17 August after the raid on Regensburg. The tail fin of Wolf's aircraft was struck by 20 mm cannon fire, whilst an errant life raft sucked out of the bomber hit its left tailplane. The top aircraft in the formation is B-17F-30-VE 42-5861 *Laden Maiden*, flown by Lt Owen D 'Cowboy' Roane. Wolf and Roane managed to reach North Africa, but nine other 100th BG Fortresses did not. *Laden Maiden* was shot down by enemy fighters during the Ludwigshafen raid of 30 December 1943 whilst being flown by Lt Marvin Leininger's crew. Only the bombardier and navigator survived and successfully evaded capture - the rest died. Decidedly war weary by the spring of 1944. *Wolf Pack* was flown back to Homestead Field, Florida, on 12 June 1944 and sold for scrap in April of the following year (Thorpe Abbotts Memorial Museum)

Left: *The Bloody Hundredth* leaving contrails high in the sky over Occupied Europe in 1944. (USAF)

Below: B-17F-85-BO 42-30063 *Picklepuss* of the 418th BS. On 17 August 1943 nine 100th BG B-17s were lost on the shuttle mission to the Messerschmitt factory at Regensburg and the legend of the 'Bloody Hundredth' was born. Bf 110s of nightfighter unit II./NJG1 attacked as Capt Robert Knox, pilot of *Picklepuss* (second from left front row) neared the target. Crews reported seeing Knox lower his undercarriage as a sign of surrender and the German fighters held their fire. Then as the 110s flew alongside, the gunners aboard the B-17 opened fire. Enraged, the Luftwaffe pilots attacked and shot the Fortress down near Aachen. (Hauptmann Hubertus von Bonin, *Kommandeur*, II./NJG1, who was leading a vic of three Bf 110s, was credited with the destruction of the B-17, which crashed with the loss of six of the crew. Four were made PoWs.). It was said that thereafter the 100th was a 'marked' group and were singled out for 'special attention'. In reality the high losses were caused mostly by poor formation flying but the 100th's bad reputation was assured. (USAF)

Above: **Smoke flares mark the target for Fortresses of the 351st BS on a rare 'gin clear' day in early 1945. Top left is B-17G-70-BO 43-37812 in the 351st BS. While returning from bombing Marburg On 23 March 1945 this aircraft crashed at Montabaur, Germany with the loss of all Lt Alfonso C. Guardino's nine man crew after it was hit by flak and then collided with B-17G-30-VE 42-97812 flown by Lt Laurence Lazzari and co pilot Gene Greenwood. Lazzari's B-17 survived with 8ft of its left wing crumpled. (Thorpe Abbotts Tower Museum)**

Inset: **The control tower at Thorpe Abbotts, now one of the finest museums of its kind. (USAF)**

Left: **B-17G-15-BO 42-31412 *Mason and Dixon* in the 351st BS was painted by Sgt Frank Stevens for original pilot Capt Floyd '*Buck*' Mason and his navigator Captain Bill Dishion. (USAF)**

303rd

BOMB GROUP

303rd Bombardment Group (H)
'Hell's Angels'
1st BD

Component Squadrons
358th, 359th, 360th and 427th Bombardment Squadrons (H)

Wartime Base
Molesworth

Operated the B-17
17 Nov. 42 - 25 Apr. 45

Total Missions
364

Total Bomb Tonnage
24,918.1 tons
(176.3 tons leaflets)

Aircraft MIA
165

Claims to Fame
Distinguished Unit Citation 11 Jan. 44

Medal of Honor:
Lt Jack W. Mathis
18 Mar. 43.
T/Sgt Forrest L. Vosler
20 Dec. 43.

Hell's Angels first B-17 in 8th AF to complete 25 missions (Jun. 43).

Knock Out Dropper first B-17 in 8th AF to complete 50 and 75 missions.

First 8th AF bomb group to complete 300 missions from UK. Flew more missions than any other 8th AF B-17 group.

Only one other group delivered a greater bomb tonnage.

Above: B-17F-40-BO 42-5264 *Yankee Doodle Dandy* of the 358th BS sustained heavy battle damage on 11 January 1944 when rocket and cannon shell fragments killed the tail gunner and a waist gunner and the pilot put the aircraft down at RAF Watton, Norfolk. *Yankee Doodle Dandy* was repaired and returned to the ZOI in April 1944 to serve at a replacement crew training base at Amarillo, Texas. It was scrapped at Stillwater, Oklahoma in 1945. (USAF)

Below: B-17Gs of the 360th BS en route to bomb transportation targets covered by their fighter shield above. (USAF)

Above and right: B-17F-25-BO 41-24577 *Hell's Angels* of the 358th BS was the first heavy bomber to complete an Eighth Air Force tour of 25 missions, between 16 October 1942 and 14 May 1943. After flying 48 missions, all without an abort. 41-24577 was flown back to the USA on 10 February 1944, having been autographed by hundreds of members of the 303rd BG at Molesworth. Once back home, it joined up with its original pilot. Capt Ira Baldwin, for a War Bond tour of industrial war plants. *Hell's Angels* was broken up for scrap at Searcey Field, in Stillwater, Oklahoma, in August 1945 (USAF)

Below: B-17G-20-VE 42-97622 *Paper Dollie* of the 358th BS, at Molesworth after crashing on 1 March 1944. Paper Dollie crashed again, at Bishop's Waltham, Hampshire on 23 July 1944 when two of Flt Officer C. M. Miller's crew were killed in action. (USAF)

Left: B-17G-50-BO 42-102453 *Princess Pat* of the 358th BS nosed over at Molesworth on 25 July 1944 when it was being flown by 2/Lt O. B. Larson. The chin turret stoved in and three of the propeller units suffered shock damage, but no one was seriously injured. (USAF via Robert M Foose)

Below left: A 358th BS Fortress is sprayed with foam after catching fire on its dispersal. (USAF)

Below: At the end of hostilities in May 1945, hundreds of aircraft wrecks still littered the countryside on the continent. This Fortress, 42-97781 BN-O *Eight Ball III*, 359th BS, came down on the edge of the Apeldoorn-Diemen Canal at Eerbeek, Holland, on 2 November 1944. Nine of Lt Jack T. Davis' crew were taken prisoner and one man was KIA. During the next year, souvenir hunters continued to strip the aircraft of parts. (Brouwer, via Ab A. Jansen)

Left: B-17F-27-BO 41-24585 *Wulf Hound* of the 360th BS and Lt Paul F. Flickinger's crew force-landed on 12 December 1942 after being shot up by the *9th Staffel, JG26*, led by Lt Otto Stammberger. *Wulf Hound* was captured virtually intact and later flown to the *Erprobungs Stelle* at Rechlin and flown on trials, whereupon it was given to the *Versuchsverband Ob d. L.* at Rangsdorf on 10 September 1943. (via Hans-Heri Stapfer)

Right: B-17G-50-BO 42-102496 *Special Delivery* of the 359th BS on 25 May 1944. This 'Fort' crash-landed at Molesworth on 18 September 1944 and was salvaged. (USAF via Robert M Foose)

Middle: *'Kicking Horse'* flown by Lt R W Cogswell returns on three engines after a raid in September 1943.

Bottom: B-17Fs of the 303rd *'Hell's Angels'* BG being bombed up at Molesworth. This scene became common throughout the countryside of central and eastern England as the 8th AF gathered strength during the summer of 1943. (USAF)

305th BOMB GROUP

305th Bombardment Group (H)
'Can Do'
1st BD

Component Squadrons
364th, 365th 366th and 422nd Bombardment Squadrons (H)

Wartime Bases
Grafton Underwood
Chelveston

Operated the B-17
17 Nov. 42 - 25 Apr. 45

Total Missions:
337

Total Bomb Tonnage
223,62.5 tons
(73 tons leaflets)
(422nd BS dropped 68 tons bombs in 8 night missions Sep./Oct. 43)

Aircraft MIA
154.

Claims to Fame
Two Distinguished Unit Citations;
4 April. 43 Paris;
11 Jan. 44
Two Medals of Honor;
1/Lt William R. Lawley Jr:
20 Feb. 44
1/Lt Edward S. Michael:
11 Apr. 44

Under Col LeMay the Group pioneered many formation and bombing procedures that became SOP in 8th AF.

422nd BS undertook first night attacks by 8th AF.

Heaviest loss of 14 October 1943 Schweinfurt mission.

Right: B-17F-55-BO 42-29529 *Nora II* of the 364th BS at Chelveston with 1/Lt Lester Personeus' crew who had flown 15 missions together and went on to finish with 25 missions apiece. *Nora II* transferred to the 384th BG and 2/L G. J. Poole crash-landed the aircraft at Grafton Underwood on unlucky 13 December 1943.
(USAF via Bill Donald)

Above: B-17G-40-DL 44-6009 *Flak Eater* of the 364th BS with shark teeth adorning the chin turret. This Fortress failed to return, landing on the continent on 4 December 1944. Subsequently repaired and flown back, she was delivered to the USA for scrapping in 1945. (USAF)

Above: B-17G-65-BO 43-37516 *Tondalayo*, 406th Night Leaflet Squadron, at Cheddington. On 4 March 1945, while returning from a NLS mission over Holland, *Tondalayo*, piloted by Lt Col Earle Aber, the Squadron CO, was set on fire off Clacton by British shore batteries which had opened up on a German intruder. *Tondalayo's* crew baled out as Aber and his co-pilot, 2/Lt Maurice Harper, remained at the controls in a desperate bid to reach the emergency field at Woodbridge. Both pilots were killed when *Tondalayo* crashed into the sea in flames. (via Mike Bailey)

Above Two B-I7Gs and B-17F-BO-50-VE 42-6174 *Home-Sick Angel/Stripped for Action* (right) of the 422nd BS prepare to take off from Chelveston. On 23 May 1945 42-6174, now named *Swing Shift*, transferred to the Night Leaflet Squadron. (USAF)

Right: Formation of 366th BS B-17s en route to their target in 1943. Bottom aircraft is B-17F-80-BO 42-29952 *Sizzle*, which was lost with 2/Lt Douglas L. Murdock's crew on the 14 October 1943 Schweinfurt mission. Leading is B-17F-27-BO 41-24592/G *Madame Betterfly*, which FTR on 6 September 1943 on the mission to Stuttgart when 2/Lt Floyd E. McSpaden had to force land at Dubendorf, Switzerland out of fuel. (USAF)

Below: B-17F MK-Y of the 366th BS over the Hüls synthetic rubber plant in the Ruhr, the most heavily defended target in the Reich at this time, near Recklinghausen on the edge of the Ruhr, 22 June 1943. The Hüls force severely damaged the plant and smoke rose as high as 17,000 ft. Production was curtailed for a month and full production was not resumed for five months after that. Sixteen B-17s were lost, ten of them shot down by *1st Gruppe JG1*. (USAF)

Right: One of the most famous entertainers to visit England in wartime was undoubtedly Bob Hope, here with singer Frances Langford and Tony Romano with Lt Ellsworth F. Kenyon's crew in the 364th BS and B-17F-95-BO 42-30242 *Lallah VIII* at Chelveston on 5 July 1943. *Lallah VIII* and Kenyon's crew FTR from the mission to Schweinfurt on 14 October 1943. Radio operator Russell J. Algren was KIA. Kenyon and eight others were made PoW. (USAF via Bill Donald)

306th
BOMB GROUP

306th Bombardment Group (H) 1st BD

Component Squadrons
367th, 368th, 369th and 423rd Bombardment Squadrons (H)

Wartime Base
Thurleigh

Operated the B-17
9 Oct 1942 - 19 Apr 45

Total Missions:
342

Total Bomb Tonnage
22,574.6 tons
(248.9 tons leaflets)

Aircraft MIA
171

Claims to Fame
Two Distinguished Unit Citations;
11 Jan 44
22 Feb 44 Bernberg

Medal of Honor:
Sgt. Maynard H. Smith
1 May 43

Oldest operational bomb group in 8th AF.

Stationed in England and at one base, longer than any other group.

First man in VIII BC to complete a tour (T/Sgt M. Roscovich 5 Apr 43).

367th BS had heaviest losses in VIII BC between Oct 42 and Aug 43.

369th BS flew for over six months in 1943 without loss.

Princess Elizabeth named *Rose of York* at Thurleigh.

Above B-I7F-1I5-BO 42-30727 *Fightin' Bitin'* piloted by Lt William C. Bisson in the 367th 'Clay Pigeons' Squadron was one of ten Fortresses the Thurleigh Group lost on 14 October 1943 over Schweinfurt. Flak knocked out two of Bisson's engines, and fighters riddled the rear fuselage, killing S/Sgt Thompson E. Wilson, the tail gunner. Only 2/Lt Charles R. Stafford, the co-pilot (who exited through the side cockpit window), and four crewmen in the aft section escaped death. (Richards Collection)

Left: B-17F-120-BO 42-30767/Y in the 367th BS crashed on take-off at Thurleigh on 5 January 1944, killing the pilot, Captain Jan R. Elliott, who was flying almost his last mission, and seven of the crew. (Richards Collection)

Below: B-17F-45-DL 42-3301 *Cavalier* of the 367th BS, after a belly landing at Thurleigh on 15 November 1943. (Joseph Minton via Larry Goldstein)

Right: B-17G-1-BO 42-31056 of the 369th BS, which belly landed at Thurleigh on 17 November 1943. Repaired, this Fortress and 2/Lt Richard S. "Calais" Wong's crew FTR from the mission to Wilhelmshaven on 3 February 1944. Three crew were KIA and seven made PoW. (Joseph Minton via Larry Goldstein)

Above: A formation of 306th BG B-17Gs is seen in early 1944. Closest to the camera is B-17G-20-BO 42-31454 *St Anthony*, which joined the 368th BS on 30 December 1943. It survived its tour of missions and was scrapped on 31 January 1946. (USAF)

Below: Lead navigator Lt Kermit B Cavedo of the 369th BS liked the numerical connection between his squadron and the '*Fightin*' 69th Regiment of World War I, so using a little literary licence, he came up with the name '*Fightin'-Bitin*' which he had applied to the nose of B-17F-50-BO 42-5426. *Fightin Bitin* was one four 306th BG B-17s lost on the raid on Kiel on 29 July 1943, when it carried I/Lt Donald R Winters crew, but both the name and the emblem, showing two insects sparring, were adopted by the 369th BS. Its sister squadron, the 367th, which had the heaviest losses in VIII BC during October 1942-August 1943, was nicknamed the '*Clay Pigeons*'. (Richards Collection)

Above: B-17F-65-DL 42-3449 of the 369th BS flown by Lt Immanuel '*Manny*' J. Klette which crashed into a wood while trying to divert, low on fuel and badly damaged, to RAF Wing, Herts, returning from the raid on Nantes on 23 September 1943. Lt Madden, the navigator, was trapped in the wreckage but he and the rest of the crew all survived the impact despite several fractures, cuts and bruises. Klette went on to complete 91 combat missions finishing the war as CO of the 324th "*Wild Hare*" BS in the 91st BG. (USAF)

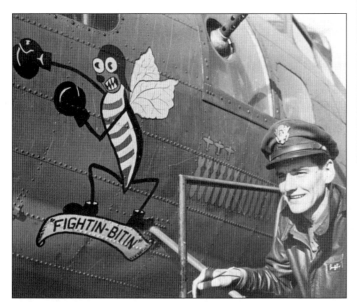

Above: B-17F-60-BO 42-29554 *Maryland My Maryland* of the 367th "Clay Pigeons" BS at Thurleigh in 1943. This aircraft was transferred to the 545th BS, 384th BG on 21 August 1943 before being sent to the ER Flight at RAF Farnborough on 19 February 1944. (via Richards)

Right: B-17G-70-BO 43-37693 dropping bombs. She was lost with 1/Lt Eldon L. Ralstin's crew on 16 August 1944 and was last seen with one engine feathered and another on fire after taking flak hits. Ralstin and his radioman were killed. Seven men survived and were made PoW. (via Richards)

Below: B-17G-55-DL 44-6583 *Commando Chief* of the 423rd BS, which later transferred to the 381st BG. (via Richards)

Below right: B-17G-60-BO *Methuselah 969 Years* (so named for its last three numbers - 42-102969) of the 367th BS, which failed to return with Lt Earl R. Barr's crew on 12 September 1944. All except two of the crew bailed out before the veteran B-17 exploded but the only casualty was the navigator, who either fell out of his chute or did not have it on when the Fortress blew up. (via Richards)

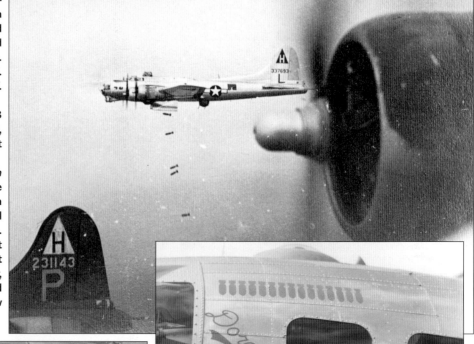

Right: 1/Lt Martin Andrews of the 423rd BS landed B-17F-25-VE 42-5841 *Est Nulla Via in Via Virtuti* (Latin for 'There is no way impossible to courage') at Magadino airfield, near Ticino, in southern Switzerland, on 6 September 1943 after running low on fuel on the Stuttgart mission. Bereft of Swiss navigation charts, 2/Lt C Gordon Bowers, navigator, relied on his silk 'escape' map to give Andrews an accurate heading to the neutral country. 42-5841 was later flown to the Emmen test and experimental centre, and at the end of the war Swiss ground crews performed an engine change before the aircraft was handed back to the AAF. (Hans-Heiri Stapfer)

Centre right: In August 1944 new group markings were applied to the vertical tails of the B-17s of the 1st Bomb Division. The 306th BG was now recognizable by a yellow horizontal band outlined in black. B-17G-70-BO 43-37715 GY-V *Lassie Come Home* and B-17G-55-BO, 42-102578 GY-D *We Promised*, which had originally served in the 398th BG, are both from the 367th Bomb Squadron. (Richards Collection)

Bottom right: B-17G-95-BO 43-38832 *Irene* taxies out in mid-February 1945 with a *Disney* bomb fixed beneath its wing. On 10 February 150 B-17s bombed targets in Holland, and during the mission *Disney* bombs, invented by Capt Edward Terrell RN, were used for the first time. Nine B-17s from the 92nd BG, led by Col James W. Wilson, dropped 18 such devices on E-boat pens at Ijmuiden. The 4500-lb bomb was powered by a rocket motor in the tail, and it was designed to pierce 20 ft of concrete before exploding. Their hefty weight prevented carriage in the bomb bay of a B-17, and so one *Disney* was carried under each wing. A single hit was recorded at the north end of the pens, and further trials were ordered, but the Allies' sweeping victories in the Low Countries, and the vast distance to suitable targets in Norway brought the *Disney* missions almost to an end. (Richards Collection)

351st
BOMB GROUP

**351st Bombardment
Group (H)
1st BD**

**Component
Squadrons**
508th, 509th, 510th and
511th Bombardment
Squadrons (H)
Wartime Base
Polebrook
Operated the B-17
14 May 1943
-
25 April 1945
Total Missions
311
Total Bomb Tonnage
20,357 (43 tons leaflets)
Aircraft MIA
124
Claims to Fame
Two Distinguished Unit
Citations;
9 Oct. 43; Anklam
11 Jan. 44

509th BS made 54
consecutive missions
Jun. 43-Jan. 44 without
loss.

'Ball Boys' Squadron
(511th BS) part of
Group.

Clark Gable flew
missions with this
group. .

Above: **Natural metal finish B-17G over occupied Europe in 1944. (USAF)**

Below: **B-17G-1-VE 42-39839 of the 511th BS, which crashed at RAF Marham, Norfolk, on 26 November 1943. This Fortress survived to the end of hostilities and in 1947 was based at Rome, New York. (Joseph Minton via Larry Goldstein)**

Identity Markings

The first B-17s arriving in the UK in 1942-43 carried the basic national insignia of a dark blue disc incorporating a white star. This was applied to the fuselage sides and left upper wing and lower right wing. The B-17Es of the first group - the 97th - also carried the words 'US Army' beneath the wings. At this time the only colour carried on the vertical tail surface was the serial number in deep yellow. For a short time the B-17 units adopted the British practice of outlining the blue disc with a 2-inch yellow band but this practice was soon abandoned in the UK.

In June 1943 white rectangles were added each side of the blue disc with the complete insignia outlined in red. Within a few months the red outline gave way to dark blue and this insignia remained standard throughout the remainder of the war and sometime afterwards.

Tactical Markings

The four B-17F groups operating during the winter of 1942-43 adopted radio call letters. These were painted in deep yellow on the vertical tail surface in letters approximately 28-30 inches high. Squadron code letters first started appearing on the B-17 fuselage sides in December 1942. These were in two letter combinations ahead of the national insignia with the individual letter aft of this insignia. These letters were usually a pale blue-grey but there were variations such as yellow and white. As new groups arrived in the UK they were all assigned squadron codes but some units never did display them and they distinguished between squadrons by other means such as coloured spinners. To aid group assembly during

the early summer of 1943, individual group letters were assigned. These were displayed against a white symbol, the First Bomb (later Air) Division using a dark blue letter within a white triangle whilst a dark blue letter within a white square was used by the Third Bomb (later Air) Division.

Early in 1944 B-17s started arriving in the UK in unpainted natural metal finish. These new arrivals used letters and air division symbols, painted either dark blue or black, with the letter within in white. In July 1944 in an attempt to further assist recognition, vertical tails were painted in various combinations of easily distinguishable colours such as red, yellow, black and blue. Some aircraft also had coloured wingtips or bands across the wing surfaces. Some groups also featured a coloured band around the forward nose section immediately aft of the Plexiglas nose cone. These markings remained standard until the end of hostilities. *Mike Bailey*

Above: **B-17F-90-BO 42-30207** *Big Red* of the 561st Bomb Squadron, 388th Bomb Group, which was lost on 27 March 1944 when 2/Lt Julius Lederman's crew FTR from the mission to Bordeaux-Merignac when a fire in the radio room spread and engulfed the aircraft. Five members of the crew bailed out safely but the ball turret gunner was killed when he fell from the plane. (Danny McGahan)

Below: B-17F-27-BO 41-24592/G *Madame Betterfly* of the 366th BS, 305th BG, which FTR on 6 September 1943 on the mission to Stuttgart when 2/Lt Floyd E. McSpaden had to force land at Dubendorf, Switzerland out of fuel. The short lived red outline to the national insignia can clearly be seen. (via Bill Donald)

Above: B-17F-10-BO 41-24487 *Eager Beaver* of the 368th 'Eager Beavers' BS, 306th BG at Thurleigh, was the longest serving B-17F in VIIIth BC, September 1942-October 1943.   It was transferred to AF Service Command on 1 May 1944, and returned to the ZOI in July 1944. It went to the Williamsport Technical Institute at Patterson Field, Ohio, on 20 June 1945. (USAF)

Below: B-17G-90-BO 43-38524 Blond Bomber II of the 710th BS, 447th BG at Rattlesden in 1944. She finished her days at Kingman, Arizona in 1945. (USAF)

B-17E 41-9043 'Peggy D' 342nd BS - 97th BG. August 1942. Grafton Underwood & Polebrook.
This aircraft took part in the Eighth Air Force's first heavy bomber mission to Rouen/Sottville on 17 August 1942. It was later used as a hack aircraft by the 381st BG. Note the armour shields on the waist guns which were later discarded as impractical.

B-17F-10-BO 41-24487 'Eager Beaver' 368th BS - 306th BG. June 1943. Thurleigh.
Shown as it was in June 1943 when the triangle was first applied to the tail surfaces. Within a few days this design gave way to the standard white solid triangle with dark blue or black 'H' within. Note the lack of astrodome on the upper nose area, typical of early B-17Fs. This aircraft also had linked twin machine guns in the nose.

B-17F-80-BO 42-30018 'Old Coffins' 532nd BS - 381st BG. July 1943. Ridgewell
This Fortress was transferred to the 305th BG in August 1943 and returned to the USA in the early summer of 1944. Note the de-icer boots have been removed in this view.

B-17F-65-BO 42-29656 'Skunkface' 322nd BS - 91st BG. Winter 1943. Bassingbourn.
Originally flown with the 303rd BG as 'Terrible Ten', this aircraft was lost on the mission to Aschersleben on 20 February 1944. Like 'Old Coffins', 'Skunkface' has the top turret modified with a higher profiled sighting window. This modification was carried out on many of the original turrets.

EIGHTH AIR FORCE B-17 TAIL MARKINGS 1945

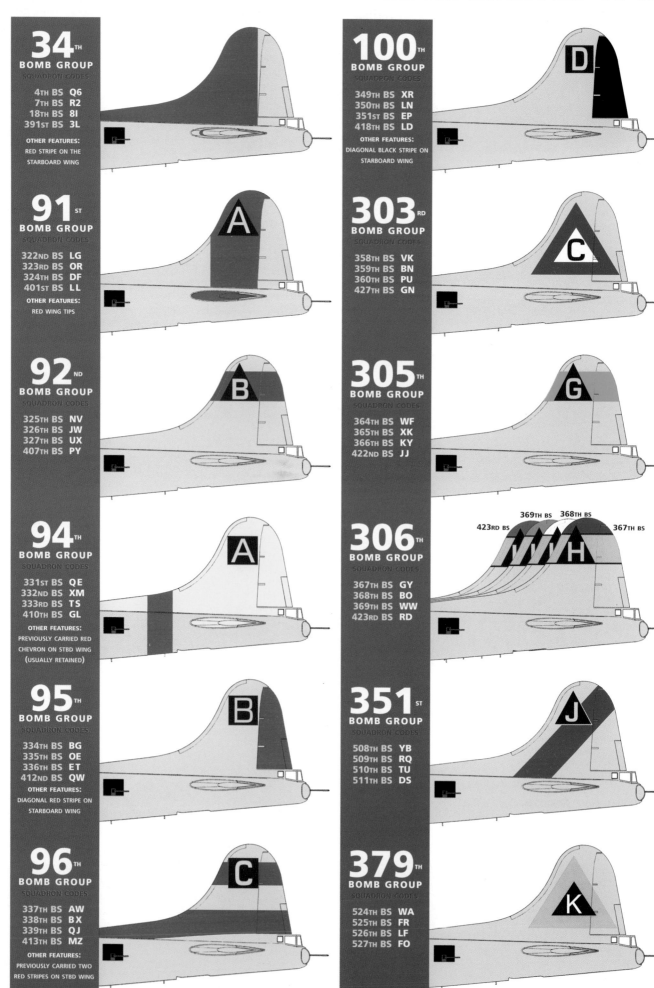

34TH BOMB GROUP
SQUADRON CODES

4TH BS	Q6
7TH BS	R2
18TH BS	8I
391ST BS	3L

OTHER FEATURES:
RED STRIPE ON THE STARBOARD WING

91ST BOMB GROUP
SQUADRON CODES

322ND BS	LG
323RD BS	OR
324TH BS	DF
401ST BS	LL

OTHER FEATURES:
RED WING TIPS

92ND BOMB GROUP
SQUADRON CODES

325TH BS	NV
326TH BS	JW
327TH BS	UX
407TH BS	PY

94TH BOMB GROUP
SQUADRON CODES

331ST BS	QE
332ND BS	XM
333RD BS	TS
410TH BS	GL

OTHER FEATURES:
PREVIOUSLY CARRIED RED CHEVRON ON STBD WING (USUALLY RETAINED)

95TH BOMB GROUP
SQUADRON CODES

334TH BS	BG
335TH BS	OE
336TH BS	ET
412ND BS	QW

OTHER FEATURES:
DIAGONAL RED STRIPE ON STARBOARD WING

96TH BOMB GROUP
SQUADRON CODES

337TH BS	AW
338TH BS	BX
339TH BS	QJ
413TH BS	MZ

OTHER FEATURES:
PREVIOUSLY CARRIED TWO RED STRIPES ON STBD WING

100TH BOMB GROUP
SQUADRON CODES

349TH BS	XR
350TH BS	LN
351ST BS	EP
418TH BS	LD

OTHER FEATURES:
DIAGONAL BLACK STRIPE ON STARBOARD WING

303RD BOMB GROUP
SQUADRON CODES

358TH BS	VK
359TH BS	BN
360TH BS	PU
427TH BS	GN

305TH BOMB GROUP
SQUADRON CODES

364TH BS	WF
365TH BS	XK
366TH BS	KY
422ND BS	JJ

306TH BOMB GROUP
SQUADRON CODES

367TH BS	GY
368TH BS	BO
369TH BS	WW
423RD BS	RD

423RD BS   369TH BS   368TH BS   367TH BS

351ST BOMB GROUP
SQUADRON CODES

508TH BS	YB
509TH BS	RQ
510TH BS	TU
511TH BS	DS

379TH BOMB GROUP
SQUADRON CODES

524TH BS	WA
525TH BS	FR
526TH BS	LF
527TH BS	FO

381st
BOMB GROUP
SQUADRON CODES

532ND BS **VE**
533RD BS **VP**
534TH BS **GD**
535TH BS **MS**

OTHER FEATURES:
RED WING TIPS

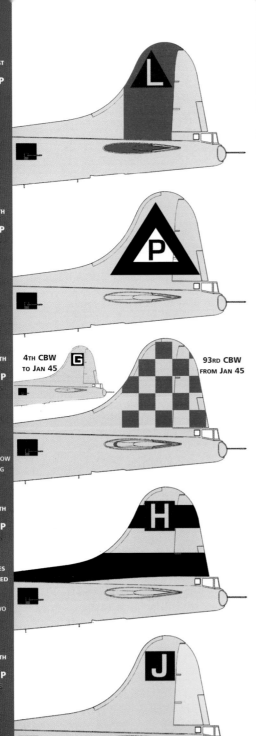

384th
BOMB GROUP
SQUADRON CODES

544TH BS **SU**
545TH BS **JD**
546TH BS **BK**
547TH BS **SO**

385th
BOMB GROUP
SQUADRON CODES

548TH BS **GX**
549TH BS **XA**
550TH BS **SG**
551ST BS **HR**

OTHER FEATURES:
PREVIOUSLY CARRIED YELLOW
CHEVRON ON STBD WING
WITH 4TH CBW

4TH CBW
TO JAN 45

93RD CBW
FROM JAN 45

388th
BOMB GROUP
SQUADRON CODES

560TH BS
561ST BS   NO
562ND BS   CODES
563RD BS   CARRIED

OTHER FEATURES:
PREVIOUSLY CARRIED TWO
BLACK STRIPES ON
STARBOARD WING

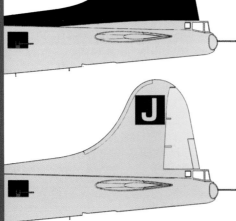

390th
BOMB GROUP
SQUADRON CODES

568TH BS **BI**
569TH BS **CC**
570TH BS **DI**
571ST BS **FC**

OTHER FEATURES:
DIAGONAL YELLOW STRIPE
ON STARBOARD WING

398th
BOMB GROUP
SQUADRON CODES

600TH BS **N8**
601ST BS **30**
602ND BS **K8**
603RD BS **N7**

OTHER FEATURES:
RED WING TIPS

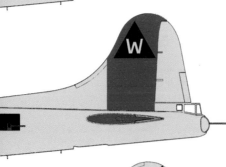

401st
BOMB GROUP
SQUADRON CODES

612TH BS **SC**
613TH BS **IN**
614TH BS **IW**
615TH BS **IY**

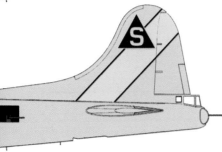

447th
BOMB GROUP
SQUADRON CODES

708TH BS **CQ**
709TH BS **IE**
710TH BS **IJ**
711TH BS **IR**

OTHER FEATURES:
PREVIOUSLY CARRIED BLUE
CHEVRON ON STBD WING

452nd
BOMB GROUP
SQUADRON CODES

728TH BS **9Z**
729TH BS **M3**
730TH BS **6K**
731ST BS **7D**

OTHER FEATURES:
PREVIOUSLY CARRIED TWO
YELLOW STRIPES ON
STARBOARD WING

457th
BOMB GROUP
SQUADRON CODES

748TH BS
749TH BS
750TH BS
751ST BS
NO CODES CARRIED

486th
BOMB GROUP
SQUADRON CODES

832TH BS **3R**
833TH BS **4N**
834TH BS **2S**
835TH BS **H8**

OTHER FEATURES:
PREVIOUSLY CARRIED
RED/BLUE CHEVRON ON
STBD WING

487th
BOMB GROUP
SQUADRON CODES

836TH BS **2G**
837TH BS **4F**
838TH BS **2C**
839TH BS **R5**

OTHER FEATURES:
PREVIOUSLY CARRIED
RED/YELLOW CHEVRON ON
STBD WING

490th
BOMB GROUP
SQUADRON CODES

848TH BS **7W**
849TH BS **W8**
850TH BS **7Q**
851ST BS **S3**

493rd
BOMB GROUP
SQUADRON CODES

860TH BS **S**
861ST BS **B**
862ND BS **C**
863RD BS **P**

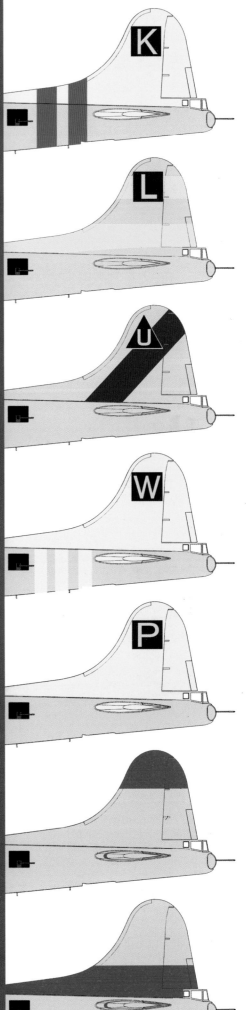

B-17F-115-BO 42-30704 *'Dinah Might'* 422nd BS - 305th BG. Chelveston.
This B-17 has her undersides painted black for night operations, (leaflets etc). The guns have been fitted with flash eliminators and flame dampers have been attached to the turbo-super-charger exhausts. Note also the three piece waist window modification. 'Dinah Might' was salvaged with severe battle damage on 17 May 1944.

B-17G-15-DL 42-37839 *'Little Willie'* 363rd BS - 388th BG. March 1944. Knettishall.
Defensively, the early B-17Gs, as shown here, didn't carry cheek guns as they were now fitted with the newly designed chin turret. All the other gun positions were the same as the B-17F. 'Little Willie' was shot down by flak on 9 March 1944 on the mission to Berlin.

B-17G-65-BO 43-37521 *'Skyway Chariot'* 351st BS - 100th BG. March 1945. Thorpe Abbotts.
A later model B-17G with the enclosed waist windows and the enlarged 'Cheyenne' tail turret, 'Skyway Chariot' was shot down by Messerschmitt 262 jet fighters on 18 March 1945 on the mission to Berlin.

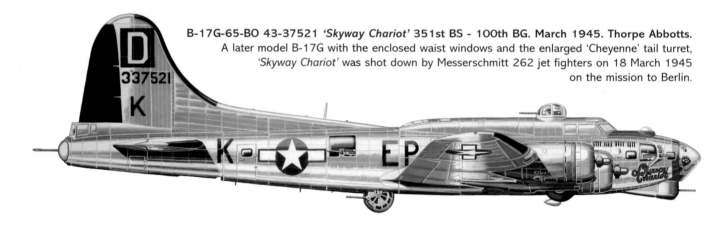

B-17G-80-BO 43-38216 *'Tempest Turner'* 862nd BS - 493rd BG. Autumn 1944. Debach.
This B-17 was named in honour of film star Lana Turner by gunner Milton Elder who, as a civilian, worked as a cameraman for M.G.M. and knew the actress well. 'Tempest Turner' was later transferred to the 34th BG and survived the war.

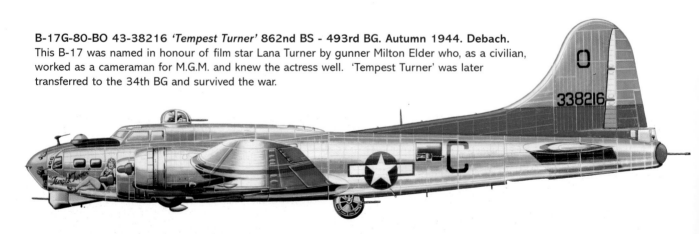

Above: B-17G 43-38837 of the 569th BS, 390th BG on its hardstand at Framlingham late in 1944. (USAF)

Below: B-17G *D-Day Doll* of the 447th Bomb Group at Lavenham, Suffolk. (USAF)

Left: A 100th BG B-17G flies low over Thorpe Abbotts in April-May 1945 during a practice release of food parcels prior to *Operation Chowhound* missions to Holland. (via Mike Faley)

Left: A 100th BG B-17G on finals to Thorpe Abbotts in typically English weather conditions. (via Mike Faley)

Left: The 100th BG was involved in the repatriation of prisoners of war and displaced persons at the end of the war. At least three of the men pictured here appear to be wearing the striped clothing of those incarcerated in Nazi concentration camps. (via Mike Faley)

Right: B-17s of the 351st BG heading for Berlin on 26 February 1945. (USAF)

Centre right: B-17G-70-BO 43-37676 of the 509th BS, dropping bombs. This aircraft crash landed on the Continent on 12 December 1944 and was salvaged in January 1945. (USAF via Ron Mackay)

Bottom: B-17G-25-DL 42-38005 *Stormy Weather* of the 509th BS which crashed at Sose Odde during a mission to Berlin on 24 May 1944. Captain Robert B. Clay and his crew were taken prisoner. (USAF)

379th

BOMB GROUP

379th Bombardment Group (H) 1st BD

Component Squadrons
524th, 525th, 526th and 527th Bombardment Squadrons (H)

Wartime Base
Kimbolton

Operated the B-17
29 May 43 - 25 Apr. 45

Total Missions
330

Total Bomb Tonnage
26,453.6 tons
(43 tons leaflets)

Aircraft MIA
141

Claims to Fame
Two Distinguished Unit Citations;
28 May 43 - 31 Jul. 44
(*operations for this period*).
11 Jan. 44

Flew more sorties than any other bomb group in 8th AF.

Dropped a greater bomb tonnage than any other group.

Lower abort rate than any other group in action from 1943.

Pioneered the 12-plane formation that became SOP during 1944.

B-17G *Ol' Gappy* flew 157 missions, probably more than any other in 8th AF.

Above: **B-17G-15-DL 42-37805** was assigned to the 525th BS at Kimbolton on 2 December 1943, where it was coded 'FR-R' and named *Carol Dawn* - it was later transferred to the 527th BS and recoded 'FO-B'. *Carol Dawn* survived the war, having twice had to put down on the continent when returning from missions, and the veteran bomber ended its days at Kingman, Arizona, in December 1945. (Charles L Brown)

Right: **HRH Princess Elizabeth with Lt Col James Dubose** (standing in for Colonel Maurice Preston) during a visit to the 379th BG at Kimbolton on 6 July 1944. Later that day Princess Elizabeth christened *Rose of York* at Thurleigh. (via Richards)

Above: A scattered trail of propaganda leaflets leads to B-17G-15-VE 42-97469 *Busy-Baby* of the 527th BS at dispersal at Kimbolton on 8 April 1944. This aircraft, which lived up to its name by enjoying a long and a varied career in the Eighth Air Force, finished up at RAF Binbrook in December 1944, where it was declared war weary on 11 January 1945. The bomber was eventually scrapped in December 1945.
(USAF via Mike Bailey)

Right: A badly wounded gunner in the 379th BG is given immediate medical treatment by the side of his Fortress at Kimbolton following the mission to Bremen on 24 June 1944. (USAF)

Above: B-17F-10-DL 42-29891 *Dangerous Dan* of the 524th BS, which crash-landed at Ubbeston, near Leiston, Suffolk on 22 December 1943 and was salvaged. (via Frank Sherman)

Left: 2/Lt Kenneth Davis, pilot of *Dangerous Dan* . Davis and his crew were shot down flying B-17F-45-DL 42-3325 *Paddy Gremlin* on 30 January 1944 when they were forced to ditch in the North Sea after being hit by fighters. All ten crew were rescued and made PoW. (via Frank Sherman)

Below: B-17F-25-DL 42-3148 *Big Bust* which first served in the 526th BS at Kimbolton and then from 30 May 1943, the 527th BS. *Big Bust* FTR from the raid on Wilhelmshaven on 11 June 1943 when Lt William F. Brinkman's crew were shot down by fighters and crashed at Marx, Germany. Eight men were KIA and two were made PoW. (USAF via Mike Bailey)

Right: General Maurice 'Mo' Preston (right) who had relinquished command of the 379th BG to Col Lewis Lyle a few days earlier, listens to Maj 'Rip' Rohr upon his return as leader of the group during the disastrous mission to Schweinfurt on 14 October 1943. The 1st BD lost 45 B-17s and the 3rd BD lost 15 Fortresses. Sixty Fortresses and 600 men were missing in total. Five B-17s crashed in England as a result of their battle-damaged condition and twelve more were destroyed in crash landings or so badly damaged that they had to be written off. Of the returning bombers, 121 required repairs. Only 88 out of the 1,222 bombs dropped actually fell on the plants and production at the Kugelfischer plant, largest of the five plants, was interrupted for only six weeks. (USAF)

Centre right: B-17G-80-BO 43-38183 *Ice Cold Katie* served with the 332nd BS, 94th BG at Bury St. Edmunds (Rougham) in July 1944 and was re-assigned to the 379th BG at Kimbolton and to the 457th BG at Glatton before returning to the ZOI at the end of the war. (USAF)

Bottom right: HM Queen Elizabeth talks with General Jimmy Doolittle while HM King George VI speaks to one of the crew of B-17G-70-BO 43-37777 *Four Of A Kind* (which obviously took its name from the last four digits of its serial number) at Kimbolton on 6 July 1944. This aircraft, which served in both the 527th and 525th Squadrons, twice failed to return when it landed on the continent in March 1945. Despite this, It was salvaged at the end of the war. (USAF)

381st
BOMB GROUP

381st Bombardment Group (H)
1st BD

Component Squadrons
532nd, 533rd, 534th and 535th Bombardment Squadrons (H)
Wartime Base
Ridgewell
Operated the B-17
22 June 1943
-
25 April 1945
Missions:
296
Total Bomb Tonnage
22,159.5 tons
(24 tons leaflets)
Aircraft MIA
131
Claims to Fame
Two Distinguished Unit Citations:
8 Oct. 43: Bremen
11 Jan.43

Highest losses of all groups on Schweinfurt mission 17 August 1943.

Above right: B-17G-35-BO 42-31968 and Lt Clarence D Wainwright's crew FTR, 24 May 1944 after a mid-air collision, near Gruental. Two German women view the crashed aircraft in which seven crew were KIA. Two men survived and were made PoW. (Ulrich Lange via Ron Mackay)

Right: B-17G-70-BO 42-37766 of the 532nd BS dropping bombs. This Fortress and 2/Lt Donald G. Henderson's crew failed to return on 25 February 1944. Six crew were KIA and four made PoW. (via Ron Mackay)

Above: B-17G-1-BO 42-31047 *Wolverine* of the 535th BS. An early G-model, it has neither cheek guns nor Plexiglas waist window panels. On its 19th mission, on 30 January 1944, *Wolverine* and 2/Lt Robert P Deering's crew failed to return from Brunswick. Eight men were killed in action and two were made PoW. (USAF via Mike Bailey)

Below: B-17G-45-DL 44-6163 *Passaic Warrior* was assigned to the 534th BS on 28 June 1944. It completed over 71 combat missions and was flown to Kingman. Arizona, for scrapping in November 1945. (USAF)

Above: B-17G-70-DL 44-6975 of the 535th BS, which bellied in at Ridgewell on 15 February 1945. This aircraft was repaired and modified as a hack with the turrets removed and extra seats fitted, for General Bill Gross, CO, 1st CBW. On 15 April 1945 this Fort was transferred to the 91st BG and flew two missions from Bassingbourn as a scout. On 25 April, now christened *Our Bridget*, she flew on the 91st BG's last combat mission of the war before returning to Ridgewell as an ETO transport for VIPs before returning to the ZOI. In 1946 *Our Bridget* became a CB-17 transport and was operated by the USN.
(Joseph Minton via Larry Goldstein)

Above and right: B-17G-45-BO 42-97174 *Joanne* of the 534th BS was engulfed in heat, flames and debris from two exploding 381st BG B-17s on the Berlin mission on 24 May 1944 which burned the fin centre section and burned off all the control surface fabric of the rudder and elevators. S/Sgt Jack R. Ross, tail gunner, bailed out over Germany when he thought that the B-17 was doomed but Lt Williams got *Joanne* safely back to Ridgewell. *Joanne* and Lt Roy H. Pendergist's crew failed to return on 21 June 1944. Two men were KIA and seven made PoW.
(via Ron Mackay)

Above: B-17G-45-BO 42-97330 *Chug-A-Lug II* of the 535th BS coming into land. This aircraft failed to return with 2/Lt Julius Levitoff's crew on 6 November 1944 when it was shot down over Germany and crashed at Rothenburg. Two men were KIA and seven made PoW. (USAF via Ron Mackay)

Below: B-17G-65-BO 43-37514/B *My Son Bob* of the 534th BS which though it twice landed on the Continent in February and March 1945, survived the war and was flown home to the USA where it was finally scrapped at Kingman, Arizona in October 1945. (via Ron Mackay)

384th

BOMB GROUP

384th Bombardment Group (H)
1st BD

Component Squadrons
544th, 545th, 546th and 547th Bombardment Squadrons (H)
Wartime Base
Grafton Underwood
Operated the B-17
22 June 1943
-
25 April 1945
Total Missions
314
Total Bomb tonnage
22,415.4 tons
(16.2 tons leaflets)
Aircraft MIA
159
Claims to Fame
Two Distinguished Unit Citations;
11 January 1944
24 April 44
Oberpfaffenhofen

Dropped last 8th AF bombs in WWII
25 April 1945.

Top right: B-17F-85-BO 42-30033 *Little America* of the 547th BS. This aircraft and Major Maurice S. Dillingham's crew FTR on 1 December 1943. One man evaded and nine were made PoW.
(via Mike Bailey)

Centre right: B-17F-65-BO 42-29723 *Wolf Pack*, which was assigned to the 546th BS, 384th BG at Grafton Underwood on 16 October 1943.
(USAF via Mike Bailey)

Bottom right: B-17G-10-DL 42-37781 *Silver Dollar* of the 546th BS, which belly landed at Grafton Underwood on 26 December 1943. After repairs *Silver Dollar* flew with the 544th and 545th Bomb Squadrons and went MIA with Lt Merlin H. Reed's crew over Berlin on 9 March 1944 when she was hit by a bomb dropped from above. Eight men were KIA and two were made PoW. (Joseph Minton via Larry Goldstein)

Above: B-17F-F-85-BO 42-30037 of the 546th BS flown by l/Lt Lykes S Henderson, is inspected by German officers after being shot down on the Villacoublay, France, mission on 26 June 1943.
(via Hans Heiri-Stapfer)

Right: B-17G-10-DL 42-37762 *Champlain's Office*, 545th BS on its belly at the naval airbase at Zwischenahn, near Bremen, 26 November 1943, one of the 25 heavies lost from the 633 aircraft dispatched. *Champlain's Office*, which was flown by 2/Lt Charles A. Zituik, was badly damaged by fighters before reaching the target, and was then 'escorted' by three Bf 109s. Zituik circled Zwischenahn aerodrome, where eight of the crew bailed out. Seven men came down safely, but ball turret gunner, Sgt Robert H. Rimmer Jr's opened 'chute caught a jackscrew in the bomb bay. Repeated attempts by 2/Lt Frank Pelley, bombardier, to pull him back on board, failed, and Rimmer was smashed to death against a hangar on the airfield which the Fortress narrowly missed during the crash-landing, at 1202 hrs. The nine survivors were taken prisoner. On board the Fortress, the Germans found the secret radio codes for 26 and 27 November 1943, and an intact *H2S* navigation radar set. (Coen Cornelissen)

Left: The crew of *Champlain's Office* (pictured in front of B-17F *Cherry*) who belly-landed at Zwischenahn airfield near Bremen on 26 November 1943 Kneeling, L-R: Sgt Clarence R. Lehmann, *tail gunner*; Sgt Florian S. Protasiewicz, *left waist gunner*; S/Sgt Lewis E. McNatt Jr., *radio operator*; Sgt. Robert H. Rimmer Jr. *ball turret gunner* (KIA 26.11.43); S/Sgt Anthony J. Roberto, *engineer*. Standing, L-R: 2/Lt Richard C. Teevan, *co-pilot*; 2/Lt Baradi, *pilot* (did not fly on the 26.11.43 mission); 2/Lt Rodney R. Helms, *navigator*; 2/Lt Frank A. Pelley Jr,. *bombardier*.
(Coen Cornelissen)

Above: B-17G-45-BO 42-97271 *Boss Lady* of the 545th BS and other "G's" en route to their target at Frankfurt. *Boss Lady* went MIA on the mission to Hamburg on 30 March 1945. One of Lt Hicks crew was KIA and eight were made PoW. (USAF)

Left: B-17G *Helena* showing the frontal gun arrangement designed to try to combat head on attacks by the Luftwaffe. (via Robert M. Foose)

Bottom: B-17G-95-BO 43-38757 *Peasely's Payoff* of the 547th BS, which despite this mishap on 8 May 1945, was repaired and returned to the ZOI where early in 1946 it was scrapped at Kingman, Arizona. (USAF)

385th
BOMB GROUP

385th Bombardment Group (H) 3rd BD

Component Squadrons
548th, 549th, 550th and 551st Bombardment Squadrons (H)
Wartime Base
Great Ashfield
Operated the B-17
17 Jul. 43 - 20 Apr. 45
Total Missions
296
Total Bomb Tonnage
18,494 tons
(184.9 tons supplies, etc)
Aircraft MIA
129
Other Op. Losses: 40
Claims to Fame
Two Distinguished Unit Citations;
17 Aug. 43: Regensburg
12 May 44: Zwickau

Led famous attack on Marienburg factory
9 Oct. 43.

Last group to be fired on - May 45: Holland.

Above: **A Fortress with its entire tail shot away plunges to earth.** (USAF)

Right: Fortresses and Liberators at Dubendorf airfield in neutral Switzerland. Nearest Fortress is flak-damaged B-17G-35-DL 42-107031 of the 550th BS, which Lt Robert G. Turner force landed at Dubendorf on 13 July 1944 during the mission to Munich. The next Fortress in line is B-17G-75-BO 42-37885 *Mrs F.D.R.* (formerly *Frostie*) of the 545th BS, 384th BG, which 2/Lt Virgil R. Broyhill force landed at Dubendorf on 24 April 1944 during the mission to Erding. In each case the Swiss interned all ten crew. (USAF)

Below: **B-17G-50-DL 44-6483/G *Ruby's Raiders* of the 550th BS** named after Ruby Newell, a WAC, named by Yank magazine as the most beautiful WAC in the ETO, which survived the war and was flown home to the USA to be scrapped at Kingman, Arizona in late 1945.

Above: **Stretcher-bearers head towards a 385th BG Fortress returning to Great Ashfield with a wounded crewman aboard on 26 July 1943. Fifteen B-17s from the group attacked Wesermünde on this date, and three were lost. Group records indicate that this aircraft was the only B-17 to return with a wounded crewman.** (M Taubkin via Ian McLachlan)

Above and right: **Lt Charles Armbruster Jr. of the 550th BS was flying B-17G-25-DL 42-38035 *Mr. Lucky* on 1 March 1945 when it was involved in a collision with another Fortress at 13,500 ft over Ostend, Belgium. The tail section was severed and with gunner Sgt Joe F. Jones (right) trapped inside, it came to earth near a farm. Amazingly, Jones survived and six weeks later he was back at Great Ashfield. All the rest of the crew were killed.** (USAF)

Above: **Colonel William B. David, 388th BG Commanding Officer from 1 February 1943 - 6 October 1944. (via Larry Goldstein)**

Below: **B-17G 'M' of the 388th BG over the sea. Note the two parallel black bands painted horizontally on the tail, which were introduced in January 1945. Two black bands were also painted cordwise on the wings (upper right and lower left). (via Ian McLachlan)**

Above and Below: **B-17G-35-VE 42-97873** *Sack Happy* **of the 563rd BS crashed on take-off for Munich on 24 February 1945. Based at Knettishall since 1 June 1944, the bomber was salvaged the following day.** (via Larry Goldstein)

Top left: B-17G-15-BO 42-31393 *SNAFU* (*Situation Normal, All Fouled Up*, although the acronym was known differently!) and its crew, led by Lt Leo Sullivan. The aircraft's original bombardier, Lt Betastas, was killed by a 20-mm shell from an enemy fighter on the Berlin mission of 8 March 1944. *SNAFU*, which was eventually renamed *Snaky*, was lost to flak on the 29 April 1944 mission to Berlin, the bomber crashing in France. Eight members of 2/Lt Donald E Walker's crew were captured, one evaded and one was killed (USAF)

Top right: B-17G *Heavens Above*. (via Larry Goldstein)

Above left: B-17F *Pegasus* with the Miller crew of the 563rd BS in front. This aircraft was followed later by a second *Pegasus* (B-17 42-31103) which the crew christened *Pegasus Too*. (via Larry Goldstein)

Above right: Lt Ranton's ten-man crew in the 563rd BS study a mission map beside B-17G-10-BO 42-31242 *Patty Jo*. This aircraft was subsequently damaged in a mid-air collision with a B-17 of the 452nd BG on 19 May 1944, its pilot crash-landing the bomber at the 453rd BG base at Old Buckenham, in Norfolk. (via Larry Goldstein)

Below: B-17G-35-DL 42-107061 *Little Joe Jr.* (formerly *Peg of My Heart*) of the 561st BS flown from Knettishall to Bodney, home of the 352nd FG in April 1944, by Lt Colonel William Chamberlain. Left is P-51B 43-7196 PZ-R of the 486th FS flown by the CO, Lt Col Luther H. Richmond (shot down and made PoW on 15 April 1944). Chamberlain was KIA soon after, on 25 May 1944. *Peg of My Heart* was lost with 2/Lt Searl G. Pickett's crew on 8 May 1944 when they were hit by fighters and crashed at Bremen. Five crew were KIA and five survived to become PoW. (Bob Sox via Bill Espie)

Above: B-17G-105-BO 43-39221 and B-17G-100-BO 43-38933 *Dear Mom* fly in close formation over the North Sea in early 1945. Having survived the war, *Dear Mom* hit a hill near Land's End during a navigational exercise on 17 May 1945, killing pilot 2/Lt H. J. Cole, co-pilot 2/Lt V. Ferguson, two navigators and two groundcrew who had come along for the ride as a makeshift engineer and radio operator. (via Robert M. Foose)

Left and above: On 20 June 1944, during the 3rd Bomb Division's mission to the synthetic oil plant at Rotensee near Magdeburg, the 388th BG lost two B-17s; the remaining aircraft aborted and returned safely. All had suffered battle damage including B-17G-65-BO 42-37523, piloted by Lt Charles Maring, which was badly crippled but returned to the field, where Maring and his co-pilot, Scott Johnson, skillfully belly-landed the Fortress without injury to the crew. Here Robert Bessett, the radio operator, and the waist gunners John Kelly and Tom Isaacs (left) examine flak holes in a shoe, while the ball turret gunner Roy Dean and tail gunner Art Woodsum right, check damage to a flak suit. Maring was killed on the mission to Merseberg, 28 September 1944, when he was Command Pilot. Lt John Hanlon, the bombardier passed out as a pilot after the war and was killed when his F-100 crashed in England in 1958. (USAF via Robert M. Foose)

390th Bombardment Group (H) 3rd BD

Component Squadrons
568th, 569th, 570th and 57lst Bombardment Squadrons (H)
Wartime Base
Framlingham
Operated the B-17
12 August 1943
-
20 April 1945
Total Missions
300
Total Bomb Tonnage
19,059.2 tons
(295.3 tons supplies, etc)
Aircraft MIA
144
Other Op. Losses: 32
Claims to Fame
Two Distinguished Unit Citations;
17Aug.43: Regensburg
14 Oct. 43: Schweinfurt

Highest claims of e/a destroyed by bomb group on one mission
(10 Oct.43).

Hewitt Dunn only man to fly 100 missions with 8th AF.

Above: Gus Mencow (3rd from left), lead navigator, 520th BS, Schweinfurt, 14 October 1943. (Mencow)
Below: B-17F-45-DL 42-3312/K *Sequatchiee* of the 570th BS, which failed to return with 2/Lt James A. Bonner's crew on 22 June 1944 when it crashed at Dreux, France. One crewman was KIA and nine made PoW. (via Ron Mackay)
Bottom: B-17G-5-VE 42-39927 *The Skillet* of the 570th BS made an emergency landing at Wormingford fighter base, in Essex, with serious battle damage in late 1943. Once repaired, it continued to serve with this group until it returned to the US in early July 1945.
(Russ Zorn via Ian McLachlan)

Top left: B-17G-30-BO 42-31892/H of the 570th BS, which went under the names of *I'll Be Around* and *The Skillet*. It was salvaged on 6 June 1944. (USAF)

Middle left: B-17F-60-DL 42-3426/Y *Kemy II* of the 571st BS, which failed to return with Lt William W. Smith's crew on 10 October 1943. (via Ian McLachlan)

Below: B-17G-5-BO 42-31 134 of the 569th BS en route to the secret German heavy water plant near the Rjukan Valley about 75 miles from Oslo on 16 November 1943. In May the following year 42-31134 was named *Gung Ho*, and on 10 September this aircraft, and Lt Charles F. McIntosh's crew, failed to return from a mission, crashing at Nuremberg. Six of the crew perished and three were captured. (USAF)

Right: During the 7 July 1944 raids against oil targets in Germany, 28 Liberators and 9 Fortresses were lost, the majority to the heavily armoured *Sturmjäger* FW 190A-8s of IV (Sturm)./JG3 and II./JG300. Two of the nine B-17Gs that failed to return, however, were lost in a tragic accident on the way in, when 42-97983 FC-Z, 571st BS, flown by 2/Lt Larue F Cribbs, and 42-10707 *North Star* of the 579th, flown by Lt Lawrence J Gregor, collided over Hoorn, the Netherlands. The smashed tail of *North Star* (shown here) plunged between the garage and the house occupied by the Sleutel family at the Westersingel. Thirteen of the 20 crewmembers from the two Fortresses, and one of the inhabitants of Hoorn, perished in the tragedy. (Jan de Groot via Ab A. Jansen)

Below: B-17G-70-DL 44-6954 of the 569th BS flown by Group CO Col Joseph A. Moller, releases its cargo of supplies to starving Dutch civilians at Valkenburg on 1 May 1945. (USAF via Mike Bailey)

398th

BOMB GROUP

398th Bombardment Group (H)
1st BD

Component squadrons
600th, 601st, 602nd and 603rd Bombardment Squadrons (H)
Wartime Base
Nuthampstead
Operated the B-17
6 May 1944
-
25 April 1945
Total Missions
195
Total Bomb Tonnage
15,781.2 tons
Aircraft MIA
58

Above: 1/Lt Lawrence M. de Lancey, incredibly, brought his crippled 398th BG Fortress back to Nuthampstead on 15 October 1944 after losing the nose, and his toggelier, Sgt George Abbott, to a direct flak hit over Cologne. (USAF)

Below: B-17G-30-VE 42-97810/S of the 602nd BS which failed to return with 2/Lt Willard G. Jacobs' crew on 9 March 1945. One man evaded and seven were made PoW.

401st
BOMB GROUP

401st Bombardment Group (H) 1st BD

Component Squadrons
612th, 613th, 614th and 615th Bombardment Squadrons (H)
Wartime Base
Deenthorpe
Operated the B-17
26 Nov. 43 - Apr. 45
Total Missions:
255
Total Bomb Tonnage
17,778.1 tons
(17.7 tons leaflets)
Aircraft MIA
95
Claims to Fame
Two Distinguished Unit Citations;
11 Jan 44
20 Feb 44 Leipzig

Second most accurate bombing in Eighth AF.

Above: B-17G-20-BO 42-31619/L *BTO in the ETO* of the 615th BS, which bellied in, was repaired, and finally lost with 2/Lt John S. Whiteman's crew at Bornholm, Denmark on 24 May 1944. (USAF)

Below: A wintry Deenthorpe on 12 January 1945. Nearest aircraft is B-17G-80-BO 43-38077 *Duke's Mixture* of the 615th BS. This aircraft was later re-assigned to the 614th BS and re-named *Tag A Long*. It finished its days at Kingman in November 1945. Behind is B-17G-60-VE 44-8371/M *Badland Bat II* (formerly *Freckles*), which failed to return with Captain Stephen J. Lozinski's crew on 16 February 1945. Eight men were KIA and one PoW. (USAF)

Left: B-17Gs of the 613th BS dropping their bombs on the target. B-17G-105-BO 43-39125/M *You All Right* (formerly *Der Grossarschvogel*) (left) and Lt Aubrey J. Bradley Jr.'s crew failed to return on 20 April 1945. (USAF)

Below: Line up of 612th BS B-17Gs at Deenthorpe. The nearest aircraft, B-17G-95-BO 43-38810 failed to return when it landed on the continent on 19 March 1945 but did finally return to the USA in 1945. Next is B-17G-43-395-BO 8733/K *I'll be Seeing You*, which crashed at Halesworth airfield on 25 March 1945 and was salvaged. (USAF)

Bottom: B-17G-40-VE 42-97938/S *Twan-n-g-g-g* of the 612th BS which crashed on 30 November 1944 and was salvaged. (via Ron Mackay)

447th
BOMB GROUP

447th Bombardment Group (H) 3rd BD

Component Squadrons
708th, 709th, 710th and 711th Bombardment Squadron (H).
Wartime Base
Rattlesden
Operated the B-17
24 Dec. 43
-
21 April 1945
Total Missions
257
Total Bomb Tonnage
17,102.9 tons
(394.9 tons supplies, etc)
Aircraft MIA
97
Other Op. Losses: 43
Claims to Fame
Medal of Honor;
2/Lt Robert E. Femoyer
2 Nov. 44.

Milk Wagon set record for 3rd AD B-17 with 129 missions and no aborts.

Above: B-17G-75-VE 44-8643/K, the nearest aircraft, survived the war and finished her days at Kingman, Arizona, in December 1945. (via Derek Smith)

Below: B-17G-40-VE 42-97976 *A Bit O'Lace* of the 709th BS. Its most famous nose art was painted by armourer Nicholas H. Fingelly who had been approached in October 1944 by the pilot, Lt John H. Bauman after his crew received permission from Milton Caniff to use the 'Miss Lace' pose from his very popular Army strip cartoon, Male Call. By the end of the war *A Bit O'Lace* had flown 83 missions. In July 1945 the bomber was flown by a skeleton crew to South Plains, in Texas, where it was stored until sold for scrap at Kingman in October 1945. (Charles E Brown)

Top left: B-17G-70-BO 43-37797 *American Beauty* of the 708th BS, which fell victim to the weather when it crashed at Rattlesden on 9 January 1945. The aircraft was repaired and continued to serve until it was scrapped in December 1945.
(via Ian McLachlan)

Inset left: B-17G-40-BO 42-97092 *Virginia Lee II* served in the 711th BS. It failed to return with Capt Keller's crew from the mission to Augsburg on 13 April 1944, landing safely in Switzerland. The B-17 had been hit in the No 4 engine by flak near the target, and shortly after crossing the Swiss border the bomber was struck again by flak. Upon landing in Switzerland the crew counted no less than 20 flak holes in their B-17.
(Herman Hetzel)

Below: B-17G-60-VE 44-8355, a PFF ship in the 710th BS flown by 2/Lt Miles S. King, takes a direct flak hit on the bomb run on 24 December 1944. Eight crew were KIA and two made PoW.
(via Derek Smith)

**452nd Bombardment
Group (H)
3rd BD**

**Component
squadrons**
728th. 729th, 730th and
731st Bombardment
Squadrons (H)
Wartime Base
Deopham Green
Operated the B-17
5 Feb. 44
-
21 Apr. 45
Total Missions
250
Total Bomb Tonnage
l6,466.6 tons
(150 tons supplies etc)
Aircraft MIA
110
Other Op losses 48
Claims to Fame
DistinguishedUnit
Citation
7 Apr. 45; Kaltenkirchen

Two Medals of Honor;
1/Lt Donald J. Gott
2/Lt William S. Metzger
9 Nov 1944

More COs (9) than any
other Bomb Group
during WW2.

Above: B-17G of the 452nd BG over Templehof, Berlin, on 29 April 1944. (USAF)

Above: On the 10 February 1944 mission to Brunswick, 29 B-17s and eight escorting fighters were lost to the ferocious German defences. Five Fortresses came down in the Netherlands, including B-17G-20-DL 42-37950 *Dinah Mite*, 731st BS, 452nd BG, piloted by 2/Lt Thomas F Sharpless, which force-landed north-east of Urk in the recently reclaimed land in the eastern Ijsselmeer (Zuider Zee), the Noordoostpolder. During the following months, the wreck was visited illegally many times by local inhabitants.
(Coen Cornelissen)

Left: Extensive battle damage to *Dinah Mite's* tail. Three of Sharpless' crew were taken prisoner, seven evaded capture.
(Coen Cornelissen)

Below: B-17Gs of the 452nd BG in formation. B-17G-55-VE 44-8249/C- of the 729th BS with *H2X* radome extended, failed to return on 24 December 1944. B-17G-70-VE 44-8518/F- went MIA on 5 December 1944. (USAF)

Above: B-17G-40-BO 42-97130 of the 731st BS. (USAF)

Below: B-17G-45-BO 42-97083 of the 782nd BS crash-landed on the German Baltic Sea coast after being hit by flak during the mission to Poznan of 11 April 1944. All ten members of the crew were captured (Hans-Heiri Stapfer)

Above: the 452nd BG leave contrails in the sky high over occupied Europe. B-17G-40-BO 42-97069 *Mon Tete Rouge II* (bottom left), of the 731st BS, failed to return from the mission to Kassel on 4 December 1944 with 2/Lt Lawrence Downy Jr's crew. Hit by flak, the bomber crashed near the German town of Bitburg, taking three crewmen with it. The remaining six were made PoWs. (USAF)

Below: B-17G-35-DL 42-107073 of the 730th BS crash-landed at Honington, in Suffolk on 30 July 1944. Subsequently repaired, it remained in AAF service until scrapped in the US in November 1945 (via Ian McLachlan)

Top right: B-17G-10-VE 42-39970 *E-rat-icator* of the 730th BS returns to Deopham Green after completing its 100th mission. This aircraft was destined to be the only original aircraft in the 452nd BG to survive the war, completing 125 missions. (Sam Young)

Middle Right: B-17G-45-BO 42-97175 *Lady Satan* of the 728th BS was lost over Strasbourg on her 85th mission, on 6 February 1945. One crewman in 2/Lt Harold G. Holland's crew was KIA and nine made PoW. (The late Marvin Barnes)

Below: B-17G-35-DL 42-107091 *Forbidden Fruit* of the 728th BS dropping bombs over Schwerte, Germany on 31 May 1944. This aircraft encountered propeller wash from another bomber on take-off on 17 February 1945 and did a barrel roll then a slow roll, before entering a flat spin and falling to earth. Only three of Joe Knoll's crew bailed out successfully. (Sam Young)

457th
BOMB GROUP

**457th Bombardment
Group (H)
1st BD**

**Component
Squadrons**
748th, 749th, 750th and
751st Bombardment
Squadrons (H)
Wartime Base
Glatton (Conington)
Operated the B-17
21 February 44
-
20 June 1945
Total Missions
237
Total Bomb Tonnage
16,915.5 tons
(142.6 tons leaflets)
Aircraft MIA
83

Above: B-17G-40-BO 42-97075 *Flak Dodger* of the 750th BS dropping its bombs. This aircraft was declared war weary in March 1945 and transferred to the 351st BG before returning home to the USA in 1945. (USAF)

Below: B-17G-30-DL 42-38113 was the 1,000th Fortress built by the Douglas Aircraft Company at Long Beach, California. It was assigned to the 750th BS where it became *Rene III* in honour of the wife of the CO, Col. James R. Luper. (see opposite page)

Top right: On 27 May, Luper nursed *Rene III* back to Glatton for a one-wheel landing after flak had badly damaged the B-17 over Ludwigshafen. On 7 October, in the same aircraft, Luper led the '*Fireball Outfit*' to Politz, where the B-17 was hit in two engines; very soon the fires spread and engulfed the starboard wing, causing the outboard engine to fall away. Seven crew, including Luper, jumped from the doomed B-17. One man baled out of the waist door, only to find his parachute on fire; he was soon engulfed in flames. *Rene III* hit the water in Stettin Bay and the bomb load exploded on impact. Three other 457th BG B-17s were lost over the target, including Luper's wingman and the deputy lead ship. Luper became a prisoner of war. Politz proved disastrous for the 457th. 38 aircraft that returned to base were badly damaged and 16 of them required sub depot repairs. Only four B-17s survived the mission unscathed. In February 1953 Luper, deputy Inspector General for Security at Strategic Air Command, was killed in a B-26 at Offutt AFB, Nebraska. (Douglas)

Right: B-17G-25-DL 42-38021/L *Mission Maid*, which served in the 748th and 751st Bomb Squadrons of the '*Fireball Outfit*', in one of the hangars at Glatton. This aircraft landed on the continent on 14 February 1945 and was salvaged. (USAF)

Bottom: A mixture of olive drab and natural metal finish B-17Gs in formation. Nearest aircraft is B-17G-35-DL 42-107026 *Hamtramack Mamma* of the 751st BS, which was lost with on the mission to Bohlen on 20 November 1944. All nine of Lt John W. White's crew were made PoW. (USAF)

Above: **Early morning mist at Glatton (Conington). (USAF)**

Above: B-17G-25-DL 42-38021 *Mission Maid* of the 748th BS. This aircraft landed on the continent on 14 February 1945 was salvaged in March 1945. (USAF)

Above: B-17G-25-DL 42-38064 *Arf n' Arf* of the 749th BS which on 23 July 1944 was rammed from behind on its hardstand by another B-17 that went out of control while taxi-ing. Another (natural metal finish) tail was subsequently used to repair the olive drab 42-38064, which failed to return with Lt Arnet L. Furr's crew on 8 November 1944 when it suffered a mid air collision in the English Channel. None of the crew survived. (USAF)

Left: B-17G-100-BO 43-38881 *Ruth Anne* of the 750th BS, which force landed on the continent on 14 February 1945 and was salvaged. (USAF)

486th
BOMB GROUP

486th Bombardment Group (H) 3rd BD

Component Squadrons
832nd, 833rd, 834th and 835th Bombardment Squadrons (H)
Wartime Base
Sudbury (Acton)
Operated the B-17
1 Aug. 44 - 21 April 45
Total Missions
188 (46 with B-24)
Total Bomb Tonnage
14,517 tons
(4.6 tons leaflets, etc.)
Aircraft MIA
33
Other Op. Losses: 24
Claims to Fame

834th BS lost no planes or personnel on first 100 missions.

Above: Lt Billy J. Woods and the crew of B-17G-75-BO 43-37942 *Blue Flippy* in the 832nd BS. This crew FTR on 8 April 1945 when *Blue Flippy* crashed at Rehau, Germany. Woods (back row far left) and Sgt Bill Rosco, nose gunner, third from right front row, were killed. The seven other crew survived and were made PoW. (Author's Collection) (see next page)

Below: B-17Gs of the 835th BS flying through flak filled skies. Bottom left is 43-37966/G, which failed to return when it landed on the continent on 5 January 1945 and was salvaged. (USAF)

Left: B-17G-75-BO 43-37942 *Blue Flippy* in the 832nd BS, which FTR on 8 April 1945 when it was shot down by flak and crashed at Rehau, Germany. (Author's Collection)

Below: B-17G-75-BO 43-37883 *Blue Streak* of the 834th BS, hurtles down in flames at Merseberg, 2 November 1944. All of 2/Lt David M. Paris's crew died. (USAF)

487th Bombardment Group (H) 3rd BD

Component Squadrons
836th, 837th, 838th and 839th Bombardment Squadrons (H)
Wartime Base
Lavenham
Operated B-17
1 August 1944
-
21 May 1945
Total Missions
185 (46 with B-24)
Total Bomb Tonnage
14,041.4 tons
(158.1 tons supplies, etc)
Aircraft MIA
48
Other Op. Losses: 37

Top left; B-17G-105-BO 43-39234 drops its bombs whilst flying over thick cloud. Assigned to the 838th BS as late as 3 March 1945, the bomber completed only a handful of missions prior to VE-Day. It was flown back to the US in July 1945 and sold for scrap five months later. (via Paul Wilson)

Above: B-17G-75-BO 43-37877 2G-E of the 836th BS on fire after a direct hit over Merseburg, Germany on 30 November 1944. The aircraft crashed at Halle. Seven of Lt Lloyd W. Kerten's crew were KIA and two were made PoW. (USAF)

Right: B-17Gs of the 837th BS and 839th BS in formation. Nearest aircraft is B-17G 45-VE 44-8023 of the 837th BS, which survived the war and was scrapped at Kingman, Arizona, in December 1945. Behind is B-17G-45-VE 44-8039 of the 836th BS, which went on to fly in the 94th BG in May 1945 and was salvaged by the 9th AF in April 1946. (USAF via Ron Mackay).

490th
BOMB GROUP

490th Bombardment Group (H) 3rd BD

Component Squadrons
848th, 849th, 850th and 851st Bombardment Squadrons (H)

Wartime Bases
Eye (Brome)

Operated B-17
27 August 1944
-
20 April 1945

Total Missions
158 (40 B-24)

Total Bomb Tonnage
12,407.4 tons
(8.9 tons leaflets, etc)

Aircraft MIA
22
Other op losses: 32

Claims to Fame
Lowest MIA losses of any 8th AF BG in combat for extended period of time.

Above: **B-17G-95-BO 43-38687 of the 848th BS at 'bombs away'. This Fortress force-landed on the Continent on Christmas Eve 1944 while returning from a raid on Frankfurt.** (via Truett Woodall)

Below: **B-17G-40-VE 42-98017** *All 'er Nothin'* **in the 849th BS crash-landed at Eye on 23 February 1945. Soon repaired, the bomber remained in the frontline force until VE-Day.** (USAF via Robert M. Foose)

Right: B-17G-75-DL 44-83254/-B *Old Doc Stork* in the 850th BS. This aircraft was assigned to the Group on 15 February 1945 and was flown in combat by Raymond E. Rosenbaum's crew. The name was suggested by the crew's ball gunner, who painted the nose art, after he saw a cartoon entitled 'Old Doc Stork'. (via Eric Swain)

Right: B-17G-75-BO 43-38024, which failed to return on 9 March 1945 when the crew were forced to land on the continent, flying through flak. (via Mike Bailey)

Below: B-17G-75-BO 43-37940 in flight. (USAF)

Left: B-17Gs of the 850th BS at Bombs Away! Nearest aircraft is *Huckleberry Juice*. (via Eric Swain)

Below: A close up of the nose of B-17G *The Judge* of the 850th BS. (via Mike Bailey)

Below: Two B-17Gs of the 851st BS leaving contrails. (via Mike Bailey)

Above: B-17G *Raidin' Maiden* in the snow at Eye (Brome) in the winter of 1944-45. (USAF)

Below: A B-17G of the 851st BS flying through flak 'thick enough to walk on'. (USAF)

Left: Lt William G Cleaves' crew, who served in the 850th BS with one of their customized leather flight jackets. Curiously, the name *Fearless Fosdick* was never applied to the aircraft. Standing in the back row, from left to right are Lts James W. Campbell (*bombardier*), Gould L. Cline (*'Mickey' operator*) and William Cleaves (*pilot*). Kneeling from left to right are S/Sgt Michael J. Lasprogato (*waist gunner*). T/Sgt Glenn L. Case (*engineer*). S/Sgt Wilbert J. Reihl (*waist gunner*) and T/Sgt James S. Collins (*radio operator*).
(via Don & Peggy Garnham)

Left: B-17G-65-VE 44-8492 of the 848th BS with its *H2X* radome extended at bombs away. (USAF)

Left: B-17G *Raidin' Maiden*. (USAF)

493rd BOMB GROUP

493rd Bombardment Group (H)
'Helton's Hellcats'
3rd BD

Component Squadrons
860th, 861st, 862nd and 863rd Bombardment Squadrons (H)
Wartime Bases
Debach
Little Walden
Operated B-17
8 September 1944
-
20 April 1945
Total Missions
156 (47 B-24)
Total Bomb Tonnage
11,733.5 tons
(3.8 tons leaflets, etc)
Aircraft MIA
41
Other op losses 31
Claims to Fame
Last 8th AF group to become operational.

Col Robert B. Landrey only man to command both fighter and bomber group in 8th AF.

Above; B-17G-65-VE 44-8452 over Haarlem during *Chowhound* food drops to the starving Dutch population on 2 May 1945 when 40 B-17s of the group dropped 3,510 cases of food. (via Truett Woodall)

Below: B-17G-50-VE 44-8200/L of the 861st BS drops its bombs in early 1945. Note the *H2X* scanner (in its extended position) fitted in place of the ball turret. This aircraft was later salvaged by the Ninth Air Force in Germany in June 1946. (via Mike Bailey)

Left: B-17G-80-BO 43-38223 was manufactured by Boeing and delivered to the AAF on 12 July The cost of this bomber was about $300,000, and each of the 51,000 employees at the Hanford Engineering Works in Seattle, Washington, gave a full day's pay to buy the aircraft. The christening ceremony the traditional breaking of a bottle over one of the propeller bosses, was performed by Mrs KB. Harris, a company employee, whose son, Lt J. E. Harris, was lost in action over Germany in April 1944. On 23 July the B-17 was flown to Hanford airport, Washington. The B-17 was then flown to Kearney, Nebraska, and assigned to the crew of Nelson W Warner for ferrying to England. On arrival, Warner's crew were sent to the 94th BG while Day's Pay was allocated to the 862nd BS and assigned to Lt Arlys D. Wineinger's crew. The first mission flown by Day's Pay was to Düsseldorf, on 9 September. Day's Pay flew more than fifty missions and then, in February 1945, following the de-activation of the 862nd BS, it was transferred to the 94th BG, where it continued flying missions until the end of the war in Europe. Day's Pay had completed 67 missions by the time it was returned to the ZOI, on 10 July 1945. (via Truett Woodall)

Right: B-17G-55-DL 44-6513 Boise Belle of the 560th BS undergoing major repairs at Debach. The bomber had suffered such severe battle damage that the front half of the aircraft was mated with the rear half of another damaged B-17. Boise Belle and Lt John E Silverman's crew failed to return from the Munich raid of 9 April 1945, the bomber having fallen victim to flak. All ten crewmen perished. (via Truett Woodall)

Left: B-17G-85-BO 43-38316 Hank's Bottle of the 860th BS came under intense fire on the mission to Merseburg on 2 November 1944 and Lt Joe Gualano was forced to make an emergency landing at St Trond, Belgium, with S/Sgt Harry Thoms dead at his left waist gun position. Hank's Bottle ended her days at Kingman, Arizona, in December 1945. (USAF via Robert M. Foose)

Above: B-17G-85-BO 43-38305/C and B-17G-50-VE 44-8200/L of the 860th BS and 861st BS let their wheels down prior to flying through the undercast and recovering at Debach in early 1945. 43-38305 caught fire on 11 March 1945 while being cleaned for nose art to be applied and was subsequently scrapped. 44-8200 survived the war and was eventually salvaged by the Ninth Air Force in Germany in June 1946. (via Mike Bailey)

Below: The mission to submarine pens at Hamburg on 30 March 1945 cost the 493rd BG three Fortresses, including B-17G-105-BO 43-39078, piloted by 2/Lt. Russell A. Goodspeed (pictured) in thc 861st BS, whose crew were on their first mission. Goodspeed returned with his No.4 engine out after taking a flak hit at the target and tried for the base at Little Walden where the right wing tip struck the ground and the B-17 broke in half at the trailing edge of the wing. The tail section remained upright and the front half of the plane skidded to a halt in a farmer's field upside down. The four airmen in the radio room were killed instantly as well as the toggelier in the nose. Goodspeed died six hours later. Only Lt Harold G. Teters, navigator, Sgt. Harry N. Davis, engineer, and Lt Roger D. Laib, co-pilot (*2nd from left front row*) survived. (Roger Laib)

EIGHTH AIR FORCE B-17 SQUADRON CODES

Code	Squadron	Code	Squadron	Code	Squadron	Code	Squadron
2C	838th BS 487th BG	CC	569th BS 390th BG	JW	326th BS 92nd BG	RQ	509th BS 351st BG
2G	836th BS 487th BG	CQ	708th BS 447th BG	K8	602nd BS 398th BG	RS	839th BS 487th BG
2S	834th BS 486th BG	DF	324th BS 9lst BG	KY	366th BS 305th BG	S	860th BS 493rd BG
3L	391st BS 34th BG	DI	570th BS 390th BG	LD	418th BS 100th BG	S3	851st BS 490th BG
3O	601st BS 398th BG	DS	511th BS 35lst BG	LF	526th BS 379th BG	SC	612th BS 401st BG
3R	832nd BS 486th BG	EP	351st BS l00th BG	LG	322nd BS 9lst BG	SG	550th BS 385th BG
4F	837th BS 487th BG	ET	336th BS 95th BG	LN	350th BS 100th BG	SO	547th BS 381st BG
4N	833rd BS 486th BG	FC	571st BS 390th BG	M3	729th BS 452nd BG	SU	544th BS 384th BG
4R	844th BS 489th BG	FL	401st BS 9lst BG	MS	535th BS 381st BG	TS	333rd BS 94th BG
6K	730th BS 452nd BG	FO	527th BS 379th BG	MZ	413th BS 96th BG	TU	510th BS 351st BG
7D	731st BS 452nd BG	FR	525th BS 379th BG	N7	603rd BS 398th BG	UX	327th BS 92nd BG
7Q	850th BS 490th BG	GD	534th BS 38lst BG	N8	600th BS 398th BG	VE	532nd BS 38lst BG
7V	752nd BS 458th BG	GL	410th BS 94th BG	NG	60th BS 493rd BG	VK	358th BS 303rd BG
7W	848th BS 490th BG	GN	427th BS 303rd BG	NV	325th BS 92nd BG	VP	533rd BS 381st BG
8I	18th BS 34th BG	GX	548th BS 385th BG	OE	335th BS 95th BG	W8	849th BS 490th BG
9Z	728th BS 452nd BG	GY	367th BS 306th BG	OR	323rd BS 91st BG	WA	524th BS 379th BG
AW	339th BS 96th BG	H8	835th BS 486th BG	P	863rd BS 493rd BG	WF	364th BS 305th BG
B	861st BS 493rd BG	HR	551st BS 385th BG	PU	360th BS 303rd BG	WW	369th BS 306th BG
BG	334th BS 95th BG	IE	709th BS 447TH BG	PY	407th BS 92nd BG	XA	549th BS 385th BG
BI	568th BS 390th BG	IJ	710th BS 447TH BG	Q6	4th BS 34th BG	XK	365th BS 305th BG
BK	546th BS 38lst BG	IN	613th BS 401st BG	QE	331st BS 94th BG	XM	332nd BS 94th BG
BN	359th BS 303rd BG	IW	614th BS 401st BG	QJ	337th BS 96th BG	XR	349th BS 100th BG
BO	368th BS 306th BG	IY	615th BS 401st BG	QW	412th BS 95th BG	YB	508th BS 351st BG
BX	338th BS 96th BG	JD	545th BS 384th BG	R2	7th BS 34th BG		
C	862nd BS 493rd BG	JJ	422nd BS 305th BG	RD	423rd BS 306th BG		

ABBREVIATIONS USED IN THIS BOOK

AAB	Army Air-Force Base	CO	Commanding Officer	MTO	Mediterranean Theatre of Op's
AD	Air Division	E/A	Enemy Aircraft	PFF	Pathfinder Force
AF	Air Force	ETO	European Theatre of Operations	PoW	Prisoner of War
BC	Bomber Command	FTR	Failed to Return	RAF	Royal Air Force
BD	Bombardment Division	HE	High explosive	VIP	Very Important Person
BG	Bombardment Group	HQ	Headquarters	USN	United States Navy
BS	Bombardment Squadron	KIA	Killed in Action	USAAF	United States Army Air Force
CBO	Combined Bomber Offensive	MIA	Missing in Action	USAF	United States Air Force
CBW	Combat Bombardment Wing	MPI	Mean Point of Impact	ZOI	Zone of the Interior

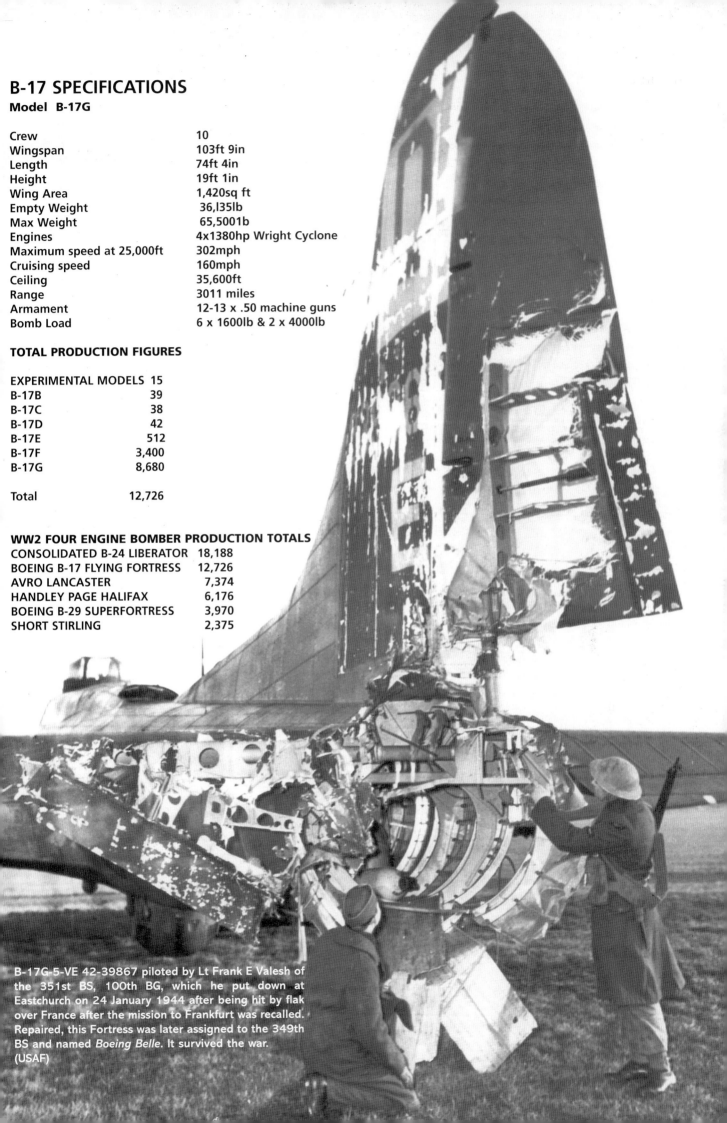

B-17 SPECIFICATIONS
Model B-17G

Crew	10
Wingspan	103ft 9in
Length	74ft 4in
Height	19ft 1in
Wing Area	1,420sq ft
Empty Weight	36,l35lb
Max Weight	65,500lb
Engines	4x1380hp Wright Cyclone
Maximum speed at 25,000ft	302mph
Cruising speed	160mph
Ceiling	35,600ft
Range	3011 miles
Armament	12-13 x .50 machine guns
Bomb Load	6 x 1600lb & 2 x 4000lb

TOTAL PRODUCTION FIGURES

EXPERIMENTAL MODELS	15
B-17B	39
B-17C	38
B-17D	42
B-17E	512
B-17F	3,400
B-17G	8,680
Total	12,726

WW2 FOUR ENGINE BOMBER PRODUCTION TOTALS

CONSOLIDATED B-24 LIBERATOR	18,188
BOEING B-17 FLYING FORTRESS	12,726
AVRO LANCASTER	7,374
HANDLEY PAGE HALIFAX	6,176
BOEING B-29 SUPERFORTRESS	3,970
SHORT STIRLING	2,375

B-17G-5-VE 42-39867 piloted by Lt Frank E Valesh of the 351st BS, 100th BG, which he put down at Eastchurch on 24 January 1944 after being hit by flak over France after the mission to Frankfurt was recalled. Repaired, this Fortress was later assigned to the 349th BS and named *Boeing Belle*. It survived the war. (USAF)

BIBLIOGRAPHY

Fortress Books

Andrews, Paul M. & Adams, William H. Heavy Bombers of the Mighty Eighth. Eighth Air Force Museum Foundation Project Bits & Pieces, 1995

Andrews, Paul M. Operational Record of the 95th Bomb Group

Barnes, Marvin E. A History of the 452nd Bomb Group Privately Published

Bendiner, Elmer Fall of the Fortresses. Putnam, 1980

Birdsall, Steve The B-17 Flying Fortress. Morgan, 1965

Birdsall, Steve Pride of Seattle: The Story of the first 300 8-17Fs. Squadron Signal, 1998

Birdsall, Steve Fighting Colors: 8-17 Flying Fortress. Squadron Signal, 1986

Birdsall, Steve Hell's Angels: 8-17 Combat Markings. Grenadier Books, 1969

Birdsall, Steve & Freeman, Roger A. Claims to Fame: The 8-17 Flying Fortress. Arms & Armour

Blakebrough, Ken The Fireball Outfit: The 457th Bomb Group.

Bowden, Ray Plane Names & Fancy Noses: The 91st Bomb Group (H) Design Oracle Partnership

Bowers, Peter M. Boeing Aircraft Since 1916. Putnam, 1966

Bowers Peter M. Fortress in The Sky. Sentry, 1976

Bowman, M.W. Four Miles High. PSL, 1992

Bowman, M.W. Flying To Glory PSL, 1992

Bowman, M.W. Castles In The Air. PSL, 1984

Bowman, M.W. Boeing 8-17 Flying Fortress. Crowood, 1998

Bowman, M.W. & Woodall, Truett Lee Jr. Heltons Hellcats: A Pictorial History of the 493rd Bomb Group. Turner, 1998

Bowman, M.W. B-17 Flying Fortress: Units of the 8thAF (Pad I & 2). Osprey, 2000 and 2002

Byers, Roland Flak Dodger. Pawpaw, 1985

Caidin, Martin Flying Forts: the 8-17 in WWII. Ballantine, 1968

Collison, Thomas Flying Fortress: The Story of the Boeing Bomber Scribner, 1943

Davis, Larry B-17 In Action. Squadron/Signal, 1984

Doherty, Robert E. & Ward, Geoffrey D. Snetterton Falcons: The 96th Bomb Group in WWII. Taylor Publishing, 1989

Ethell, Jeffrey L & Simonsen, Clarence The History of Aircraft Nose Art WWI to Today Motorbooks, 1991

Freeman, Roger A. 8-17 Fortress At War Ian Allan Ltd 1977

Freeman, Roger A. with David Osborne The B-17 Flying Fortress Story. Arms & Armour, 1998.

Freeman, Roger A. The Mighty Eighth. MacDonald, 1970

Freeman, Roger A. The Mighty Eighth In Art. Arms & Armour, 1996

Freeman, Roger A. Airfields of the Eighth - Then and Now. After the Battle, 1978

Freeman, Roger A. Mighty Eighth War Manual. Jane's, 1984

Good Brown, James The Mighty Men of the 351st - Heroes All Publishers Press, 1984

Havelaar, Marion H. with Hess, William N. The Ragged Irregulars of Bassingbourn. Schiffer

Hawkins, Ian L. B-17s Over Berlin: Personal: Stories from the 95th Bomb Group (H). Brasseys, 1990

Hess, William B17 Flying Fortress. Ballentine 1974

Huntzinger, Edward J. The 388th At War 1979

Jablonski, Edward Flying Fortress. Doubleday

Johnsen, Fred Winged Majesty. PNAHF 1980

Kurtz, Margo My Rival The Sky. Putnam, 1945

La Strange, Richard, Century Bombers: The Story of the Bloody Hundredth

McDowell, Ernest R. Flying Fortress in Action. Squadron Signal, 1987

MacKay, Ron. 351st Bomb Group.

Rust, Kenn C. Eighth Air Force Story, WWII.

Scutts, Jerry B-17 Flying Fortress.

Slater, Harry E. Lingering Contrails of The Big Square A. 94th Bomb Group (H) 1942-45

Smith Jnr, Ben Chick's Crew:

Smith, John N. Airfield Focus 37: Deenthorpe 42 44: Grafton Underwood. GMS, 1999-2001

Strong, Russell A. First Over Germany: 306th BG

34th Bomb Group (H) Turner Publishing

The Story of the 390th Bomb Group (H).

Varnedoe, W.W. Jr. B-17s of the 385th Bomb Group